The Chosen Fast
And
Prayer

Robert P. Holland

Editing by Ron Lewis

ISBN: 1-4664-8563-9
ISBN-13: 9781466485631

Dedication

This book is dedicated to my wife and companion in ministry, Dolly. I don't have words to express my love and appreciation for her support for me and the ministry. At our wedding, when she said, "I will" to the question for better or for worse, she meant every word. I made some bad decisions that cost us dearly, but she never complained about the hardships brought on as a result of the bad decisions. She always made the best of the circumstances.

She has always been by my side in ministry. I am thankful for the gift of encouragement that the Holy Spirit has given to her. Not only have I benefitted from it, but many others have as well. She is truly a gift to me from my heavenly Father.

Prologue

Instructions for fasting in the Old Testament are called the fast chosen by the LORD—the **Chosen Fast** (Isaiah 58:6–14). While the phrase **Chosen Fast** isn't found in the New Testament much of the teaching in the Gospels and Epistles are instructions for practicing the **Chosen Fast:** (1) **Love the Neighbor**, (2) **Promises**, and (3) **Love the LORD**. The three functions are a microcosm of the Old Testament Covenant the Lord made with Israel at Mount Sinai.

A covenant is an agreement between the Lord and his people. He promises to do certain things and asks them to do certain things. In the **Chosen Fast,** the people are asked to **Love their neighbor** and **Love the LORD**. Obeying the commandments is **Wisdom**. In return, the **Lord** gives them **Promises. Wisdom + Promise = Covenant**. Faith in the Lord's faithfulness to give us the **Promises** without being faithful to his commandments isn't **Covenant**. It is **Promise ≠ Covenant**.

Promises aren't received by asking the Lord for them, trusting him to give them to us, or confessing them. They are the life that emanates from obeying his commandments—**Wisdom**. Therefore we don't go to the Bible and look up a certain promise, see what the commandment is to receive it, and then obey the commandment to receive the promise. Rather **Wisdom** and **Promises** are a daily lifestyle of obeying the commandments and the **Lord** giving us the promises we need (Isaiah 58:6–14; Matt. 6:33; Phil. 4:19). The combination is fellowship with God, giving and receiving grace.

Practicing the **Chosen Fast** transforms the way we pray—from a set period of time to **24/7/365**. It is a change of focus from our self to others, from asking to giving thanks, and listening. It is an entirely different way of living.

Teaching in the New Testament of the Lord Jesus Christ's return is immediately followed by instruction for living until He returns. Practicing the Chosen Fast is following those instructions and living in the kingdom of heaven until He returns.

Contents

Foreword   ix
Chapter I   Fasting — Old and New
               Testaments   I
               Public Fasts —Old Testament   3
               Individual Fasts — Old Testament3
               Forty Day Fasts —
                   Old and New Testaments   5

Chapter 2   Traditional Fast   7
               Weekly   10

Chapter 3   Daniel Fast   15
               24/7/365   18
               Twenty-One Days   22

Chapter 4   Chosen Fast   25
               Love the Neighbor   28
               Promises   34
               Love the Lord   36
               24/7/365   51

Chapter 5   Chosen Fast and Prayer   57
               Prayer Bloopers   60
               Asking   70
               Listening   73

Chapter 6   Chosen Fast and Matthew 25   85

Foreword

Over the years, I have observed firsthand the ministry of Robert P. Holland, associate pastor of the First Assembly of God in Parkersburg, West Virginia. His deep love for Jesus Christ, his faithfulness to the church and to the Lord, and his ministries to the sick and to new Christians have always impressed me.

I am impressed once again after having read his new booklet about the **Chosen Fast** and **Prayer**. His treatment of the topic is quite thorough and enlightening, covering both the Old and New Testaments and going beyond the merely superficial aspects of fasting.

Both new and mature Christians will greatly benefit from this little volume. They will learn from Biblical examples that not only are Christians to fast under the New Covenant but that there are right ways and wrong ways to fast. Many believers think that there are only one or two reasons to fast such, as averting judgment or seeking answers to specific prayers, but Pastor Holland shows that there are many reasons why people in the Bible fasted.

He explores the many false assumptions that Christians have about fasting. Furthermore, he gives Biblical evidence that not all fasts require total abstinence from food. We get a clear picture of the many advantages of fasting for modern-day Christians but, much more importantly, we learn how fasting is connected to seeking God and his righteousness, to maintaining joy in our spiritual lives, to ministering to the lost and sick, and to the gaining of wisdom, which begins with a reverential awe toward God our Father.

Brother Holland masterfully compares and contrasts the chosen fast with the traditional fast as well as public fasts with individual fasts and shows how these are related to prayers of praise and the acts of asking and listening. The chosen fast in particular, spiritually understood as wisdom in its highest form, causes us to not only know what Jesus wants of us but causes us to lovingly obey him and follow him in our daily lives. After reading this gem of a work, readers will be inspired to make fasting a regular part of their spiritual discipline and devotion. I know it has in mine.

Randy Oldaker

September 23, 2011

Randy Oldaker is a full professor of ancient and modern languages at West Virginia University at Parkersburg (WVUP). At WVUP, Professor Oldaker is actively involved as a member of the university's Social Justice Committee, a member of the Internationalization Committee, and faculty advisor of Chi Alpha Christian Ministry and the Multicultural Awareness Coalition.

He is a member of the First Assembly of God in Parkersburg, West Virginia, where he teaches one of the adult Sunday school classes and serves the Appalachian District in its School of Ministry a few times per year, teaching the history of the Christian church, Biblical history and geography, and Old and New Testament survey courses.

Chapter 1
Fasting—Old and New Testaments

Although there is no commandment in the New Testament to fast, Jesus assumed his followers would fast when he said, "Moreover, when ye fast..." (Matt. 6:16) When Jesus and his disciples were criticized for not fasting, he replied, "Can the children of the bridegroom mourn, as long as the bridegroom is with them? but the days will come, when the bridegroom shall be taken away from them, and then shall they fast" (Matt. 9:15). And they did fast:

As they ministered to the Lord, and fasted, the Holy Ghost said, Separate me Barnabas and Saul for the work whereunto I have called them. And when they had fasted and prayed, and laid their hands on them, they sent them away (Acts 13:2, 3).

And when they had ordained them elders in every church, and had prayed with fasting, they commended them to the Lord, in whom they had believed (Acts 14:23).

Defraud ye not one the other, except it be with consent for a time, that you may give yourself to fasting and prayer (1 Cor. 7:5).

In the Old Testament, the LORD criticized Israel for the way they were fasting (Isaiah 58:3b–5 NKJV).

"In fact, in the day of your fast you find pleasure, and exploit all your labors. In deed you fast for strife and debate, and to strike with the fist of wickedness. You will not fast as you do this day, to make your voice heard on high. Is it a fast that I have chosen, a day for a man to afflict his soul? Is it to bow his head like a bulrush, and to spread out sackcloth and ashes? Would you call this a fast, and an acceptable day to the Lord?"

Jesus criticized people for the way they were fasting. "Moreover, when ye fast, be not, as the hypocrites, of a sad countenance: for they disfigure their faces, that they may appear unto men to fast. Verily I say unto you, They have their reward" (Matt. 6:16).

Fasting isn't making ourselves miserable, as Israel did to get the Lord's attention (Isaiah 58:5), neither is it having a sad countenance as the hypocrites did to get the people's attention (Matt. 6:16). Rather, it is hungering and thirsting after righteousness (Matt. 5:6), the desire to love the Lord with all our heart, soul, and mind, and our neighbor as ourselves (Matt. 22:37–39).

There is one place in the Old Testament where the LORD gave instructions for fasting (Isaiah 58:6–14). It isn't a commandment, but instructions for living in a personal covenant relationship with the LORD. It is called the fast chosen by the LORD, often referred to as the **Chosen Fast**. Although Jesus didn't give a commandment in the New Testament to fast, a considerable amount of his teaching and that of other New Testament writers are practical applications for practicing the **Chosen Fast**.

Public Fasts—Old Testament

Public fasts were called in times of peril. When the nations came to battle against Jehoshaphat in Jerusalem, he called for a fast (2 Chron. 20:1–3). After Jonah proclaimed doom to the city of Nineveh, the king called for a fast of both people and animals (Jonah 3:6–8). Esther called for a three-day fast when she was informed that Haman had conspired to destroy all the Jews in the kingdom (Esther 4:15). In the time of a locust plague, the people were called to fast (Joel 1:14).

Following defeat, a public fast was called for repentance and mourning. During a two-day battle of Israel against Benjamin, Israel lost forty thousand men. "Then all the people of Israel, and all the people, went up, and came into the house of God, and wept, and sat there before the Lord, and fasted that day until evening, and offered burnt offerings and peace offerings before the Lord" (Judges 20:26). When the ark of the Lord was taken away by the men of Kirjath Jearim, Samuel called for a fast to mourn and repent (1 Sam. 7:1–6). When Saul and Jonathan were killed, David and his men mourned and wept and fasted until evening (2 Sam. 1:11).

Fasting in the times of a national crisis or defeat is a common human response just as it is in the time of sickness. In life-threatening situations, we have no desire to eat.

Individual Fasts—Old Testament

In addition to pubic fasts, there were individual fasts. David fasting when his son by Bathsheba was gravely ill gives us some insight into his reasoning for the individual fast. He fasted until the child died. Then he arose from the ground, washed and anointed himself, and changed his clothes. He went into the house of the Lord and worshiped. Then he went to his own house, and when he requested, they set food before him, and he ate.

He explained to his servants why he fasted. "While the child was yet alive, I fasted and wept: for I said, Who can tell whether God will be gracious to me, that the child may live?' But now he is dead, wherefore should I fast? can I bring him back again? I shall go to him, but he shall not return to me" (2 Sam. 12:2).

Another account of an individual fast is found in the book of Daniel. He mourned three full weeks. During that time, he ate no pleasant food, no meat or wine came into his mouth, nor did he anoint himself at all, till three whole weeks were fulfilled (Daniel 10:2, 3). Following the fast, he received a vision of what would transpire with the nation of Israel in the latter days (v. 14).

Right away, one important difference emerges between the fast of David and that of Daniel. David didn't eat while fasting, but Daniel did. He called the food he ate unpleasant. He ate no meat or drank any wine (Dan. 10: 2, 3). The word translated "vegetable" in Daniel 1:12 (NKJV) and "pulse" (KJV) and the one translated "food" in Daniel 10:3 (NKJV) and "bread" (KJV) are two different words, but carefully studying the two verses, we can conclude that the unpleasant food in Daniel 10:3 was the same as the vegetables in Daniel 1:12.

The Hebrew word translated vegetables in Daniel 1:12 comes from the word for seed. "And God said, 'Behold, I have given you every herb bearing seed, which is upon the face of all the earth, and every tree, in the which is the fruit of a tree yielding seed; to you it shall be for meat'" (Gen. 1:29). Fruits, vegetables, nuts, and grains are all from seed. So Daniel's food during his twenty-one days of fasting may have included fruits, nuts, and grains as well as vegetables.

David's fast was for his infant son by Bathsheba who was gravely ill. In such crisis, few people have a desire to eat, but Daniel's fast was to hear from the Lord concerning the future of the nation of Israel. They were exiles in Babylon at that time. While waiting to hear from the Lord, Daniel would no doubt have gotten hungry. The fast lasted twenty-one days (Daniel 10:12–14). From these two individual fasts, we also observe the similarities found in the public fasts: times of peril and waiting before the Lord for wisdom.

Forty-Day Fasts—Old and New Testaments

Moses fasted forty days while on Mount Sinai receiving instructions from the LORD for Israel to be a kingdom of priests and a holy nation (Exodus 19:6).

Elijah fasted forty days before he heard the still small voice of the Lord telling him to anoint Hazael as king of Syria, Jehu king over Israel, and Elisha to be his successor (1 Kings 19:5–16).

When Jesus had fasted forty days and forty nights, the tempter came to him. (Matt. 4:1–11).

Chapter 2
Traditional Fast

Many people think of going without food when they hear the word fasting. Therefore, I am using the phrase **Traditional Fast** for abstaining from food in order to distinguish it from the **Daniel Fast** and the **Chosen Fast** during which time people do eat. A casual reading of fasting in the Old Testament has resulted in two false assumptions about the **Traditional Fast**: (1) fasting is only for a time of crisis in our life, and (2) denying ourselves food earns the Lord's favor. While the above fasts in the Old Testament were in the times of crisis, the fasts in the New Testament weren't (Acts 13:2, 3; 14:23; 1 Cor. 7:5). Neither is the **Chosen Fast** in a time of crisis for the person practicing it.

A careful reading of the Old Testament fasts mentioned in the last chapter reveal that they weren't to earn the Lord's favor. The fast by the king of Nineveh and his people was genuine repentance for their sins. Jonah was angry because the Lord was gracious and forgave them rather than punish them (Jonah 4:2). In Jonah's opinion, they should never have received the Lord's grace, mercy, and lovingkindness. Both Esther and Jehoshaphat called on others to fast with them in the time of their crisis in order to receive wisdom from the Lord. They didn't know what to do, but they looked to the Lord who did. By fasting, they gave their complete attention to listening for his instructions. They weren't trying to get his attention or earn his favor.

The Lord gave both Jehoshaphat and Esther wisdom. Esther went before the king. He received her and granted her request. Haman was hanged on the gallows he had built to hang Mordecai (Esther 7:10). The nations that came against Jehoshaphat were defeated by the Lord. Israel didn't have to fight in the battle; the Lord fought for them. The king sent the singers before the army.

In the Book of Joel, the prophet called the people to fast, repent, and return to the Lord (2:12–18). Israel had been warned that if they turned away from the Lord and his law, one of the consequences would be locust plagues (1 Kings 8:37–40). If they repented and returned to the Lord, He would be merciful to Israel.

Fasting and looking to the Lord in the time of a crisis resulted in peace, joy, and strength rather than panic, idolatry, and weakness: (1) Peace "You will keep him in perfect peace, whose mind is stayed on You, because he trusts in You," (Isaiah 26:3 NKJV); (2) Joy (the person whose mind in stayed on the Lord is in his presence, and in his presence is fullness of joy, (Psalm 16:11); (3) Strength (the person who is looking to the Lord and is in his presence is waiting upon the Lord). And "they that wait upon the Lord shall renew their strength" (Isaiah 40:31).

When we practice the **Traditional Fast** in the time of a crisis or in the time of defeat, we usually don't want to eat. But when we practice it and there is no crisis, we do want to eat. Not eating when we are hungry requires self-control. If we can exercise self-control over the desire for food, we can exercise self-control over other areas of our life. Therefore, the Traditional Fast helps us overcome addictions so that we may live in freedom experiencing the power of the crucifixion and resurrection of Jesus Christ in our life. "I am crucified with Christ: nevertheless I live; yet not I, but Christ liveth in me: and the life which I now live in the flesh I live by the faith of the Son of God, who loved me, and gave himself for me" (Gal. 2:20). Our spirit is in control and not our appetite.

In addition to self-control, the Traditional Fast helps us to better understand something of the hunger that millions around the world experience daily. Listening for the Lord to speak gives us an opportunity to receive instructions from him to help feed the hungry in America as well as in other countries.

Early in my Christian life, I understood enough about fasting from reading through the Bible to start fasting one day each week. I still remember my first day of fasting; it was during the week. Where I worked, we took a morning coffee and donut break. The person who went to the cafeteria for coffee and donuts was chosen by the toss of a coin.

I liked coffee and donuts—it was more than like. I was addicted to them. So, when I said I didn't want any coffee or donuts, it was as though the person taking the order couldn't believe what he was hearing. From reading about fasting in the Scriptures, I knew I wasn't to tell people I was fasting. It was between me and the Lord, but I wasn't prepared for the questions. "Why?" "I just don't want anything today." "Are you sick?" "No. I just don't want anything today."

The conversation at the coffee break focused on me not having coffee and donuts. It got even more intense at lunch. "No lunch!" Many people seem to think that if we don't eat at least three meals a day, we're going to starve. Before the day was over, my coworkers came to the conclusion that I was fasting.

I didn't know it at the time, but fasting was one of the most important steps I could have taken to mature in my Christian life. It helped me develop self-control, appreciate food, overcome my addiction to junk food, look beyond my needs to the needs of others, minister and intercede for them, repent, and confess my sins.

Through the years, I have fasted on different days of the week. In the 1970's, I joined with other Christians who took every Friday for prayer and fasting for our troops in Vietnam. In April of 1995, Rev. Thomas Trask, the general superintendent of the Assemblies of God, was the speaker at the District Council in Roanoke, Virginia. One morning during council, he shared with those in attendance the importance of fasting. He had asked everyone at General Council headquarters in Springfield, Missouri, to fast on Tuesdays, and he asked the pastors at the District Council and their congregations to also join them on Tuesdays for a day of prayer and fasting. I accepted the challenge.

Weekly

Adversity was a cause for calling a fast in the Old Testament. It is also a cause for us to keep the **Traditional Fast** one day weekly. Two adversities confronting America are threats of a terrorist attack and the breakdown of moral standards that threatens the collapse of the traditional family as we know it in America. It is also a time to look beyond America to the adversity of our brothers and sisters in Christ who are being persecuted in several countries, millions who are hungry, and the slave trade of young girls for prostitution, to name a few.

There are ever-occurring disasters around the world: floods, earthquakes, wars, volcanic eruptions, droughts, tornadoes, cyclones, hurricanes, tidal waves, and so many other things that are too numerous to mention. Fasting and prayer goes beyond asking the Lord to intervene on behalf of others to making ourselves available to help—giving to feed the hungry, buying back girls who are sold into slavery, providing financial help for Christian families in other countries who are going through severe persecution, etc.

After a disaster, the Israelites would call for a day of fasting to repent and mourn. They acknowledged their sins as the cause of the disasters. They had broken the covenant the Lord had made with them and were worshiping other gods. The Book of Judges is a sad account of the cycle of turning away, disaster, repentance, and mourning.

The one-day weekly fast provides a time of repentance and mourning for the moral failures making headlines daily in America: murder and rape of children, greed that wipes out people's savings and pensions, the collapse of the housing market, hundreds of thousands of people losing their homes and jobs, Christians choosing to disobey the commandments and break up families, college students who are swayed from their faith by the secular campus classroom teaching, and campus lifestyles are only a few causes for mourning. Repentance and mourning, not because we committed the crimes, but because we live in the country where they take place. The moral failures remind us of our sins of which we need to repent: failure to pray and witness to the lost, and becoming hardened to the suffering of others.

Moses fasted forty days while on Mount Sinai receiving instructions from the LORD for Israel to be a kingdom of priests and a holy nation. Christians are called by the Lord to be the same (I Peter 2:9). The one-day weekly fast provides us an opportunity to meditate upon what it means to be a kingdom of priests and a holy nation. Since the kingdom of priests and the holy nation are directly related to the Commandments, the one-day fast is also a time to meditate upon what it means to delight in the Commandments and to delight in the Lord.

Elijah fasted forty days and heard the still small voice of the Lord instructing him to anoint Hazael as king of Syria, Jehu king over Israel, and Elisha as his successor (I Kings 19:5–16). The one-day weekly fast is a time of listening for the still small voice of the Lord to initiate national and international changes both secular and sacred, starting with us (Isaiah 6:8).

When Jesus had fasted forty days, the tempter tried to turn him away from his mission to save the world. The one-day fast each week is a time to receive power to overcome temptations that try to turn us away from bringing salvation to the world. The disciples were fasting and praying when the Lord said, "Separate now for me Barnabas and Paul for the work to which I have called them." We read of all the ways the Lord used Paul and Barnabas to reach people with the gospel.

Paul fasted three days after his conversion, and the Lord sent Ananias with a message to Paul that he was to carry the gospel to the nations. He was obedient, and much of the New Testament is about his ministry and what can happen when we are fasting and praying to be used of the Lord to reach the world with the gospel. It can take place when we understand John 3:16 not just to save us, as wonderful as that is, but let it become God's love in us for the salvation of the world. It begins where we are as we pray, minister, and give to support missions around the world.

Chapter 3
The Daniel Fast

Daniel chose to eat vegetables and drink water rather than eat the king's meat and drink his wine (Dan. 1:12, 10:3). He was living in Babylonian exile with other Jews, and he didn't want to defile himself with the king's food and wine. He didn't want to break the Jewish food laws and eat something that wasn't kosher. He wanted to maintain his Jewish lifestyle in a foreign land. He chose not to be conformed to the Babylonian lifestyle, and he maintained the diet for three years while he was in training to serve in the king's palace.

Not only did Daniel follow that diet for three years, but Shadrach, Meshach, and Abed-Nego did as well. After the three years of training, the king interviewed all of the students and none among them were like Daniel, Shadrach, Meshach, and Abed-Nego. Therefore, they served before the king. "And in all matters of wisdom and understanding, that the king inquired of them, he found them ten times better than all the magicians and astrologers that were in all his realm" (Dan. 1:20).

It is important to recognize that while Daniel, Shadrach, Meshach, and Abed-Nego didn't conform to the Babylonian lifestyle, they were superior servants to the king and the people of Babylon. They obeyed the laws of the land except when the law demanded them to disobey the law of the Lord; then they chose death rather than to obey the laws of the land.

Because they obeyed the Lord's commandment rather than bow down to an idol, Shadrach, Meshach, and Abed-Nego were cast into the fiery furnace. They chose death rather than break the first commandment, "Thou shalt have no other gods before me" (Exodus 20:3). The Lord delivered them, and the king and all his officials witnessed his power. Then the king promoted Shadrach, Meshach, and Abed-Nego in the province of Babylon (Dan. 3:16–30).

The enemies of Daniel instigated a law that banned anyone from praying to any god or man for thirty days. The person who disobeyed the law would be cast into a den of lions. Daniel's enemies knew that he was faithful to his God and wouldn't obey the law. Daniel chose to disobey the law and pray to the Lord even though it meant death. Life for Daniel was to love the Lord—obey his commandments (Deut. 30:19, 20). Death was disobeying the commandments of the Lord. Therefore he chose to die and live rather than live and be dead.

Daniel was thrown into the lions' den, but the Lord delivered him. Then King Darius made a degree, "That in every dominion of my kingdom men tremble and fear before the God of Daniel: for he is the living God, and steadfast forever, and his kingdom that which shall not be destroyed, and his dominion shall be even unto the end" (Dan. 6:26).

Daniel inspired future generations of both Jews and Christians. When Antiochus IV (175–164 BC), called Antiochus Epiphanes, ("the Manifest [God]"), issued an edict to the effect that throughout his kingdom all people should be one in religion, law, and custom, among the Jews, there were those like Daniel that would not submit.[1] Many became martyrs. The same was true of the Christians under Roman rule. The same is true of Christians today in China, Iran, Iraq, Indonesia, Pakistan, India, Sudan, Congo, North Korea, and Vietnam, to mention some.

Mehdi Dibaj was born into a prosperous Iranian family and received Christ as Savior as a teenager after reading a gospel tract. He was scheduled for execution after ten years of imprisonment for converting to Christianity. During his imprisonment, he endured unending pressures to recant his faith, including two years of solitary confinement in a cage too small to lie down in or stand up. He also suffered numerous beatings and mock executions.

In his written defense for his court trial on December 3, 1993, Mehdi wrote: "Life for me is an opportunity to serve Him, and death is a better opportunity to be with Christ. Therefore, I am not only satisfied to be in prison for the honor of His holy name, but I am ready to give my life for the sake of Jesus my Lord and enter His kingdom sooner, the place where the elect of God enter everlasting life."

In 1994, Haik Hovsepian, general superintendent of the Iran Assemblies of God, valiantly and boldly appealed to the world on behalf of Mehdi. Haik's appeal was effective. Mehdi was released from prison on Jan. 16. Only two days later Haik was tortured and murdered. Just six months after release from prison, Mehdi's body was found in an alley. He had been stabbed multiple times, and his assassin was never identified.[2]

Not only did Daniel choose to eat vegetables and not be conformed to the Babylonian lifestyle, but he also continued in prayer for twenty-one days eating no pleasant food as he waited for the Lord to give him information concerning Israel in the latter days. He was fasting, but he ate fruit and vegetables (Daniel 10:2, 3).

For people who are unable to practice the **Traditional Fast** because of health problems, the **Daniel Fast** offers an alternative. But check with a physician first. Alternatives for the **Traditional Fast** (going without food) are: replace time spent watching TV, Internet, sports, and other leisurely activities with prayer, intercession, reading, and meditating upon the Scriptures for instructions to minister and witness to others.

24/7/365

Unlike Daniel, Christians aren't bound by the Jewish food laws. Jesus declared all food clean (Mark 7:14–16). But like Daniel, there are Christians who choose to live the Christian lifestyle in a non-Christian environment. So the **Daniel Fast** for a Christian is twofold—**a set period of time** and **an indefinite period of time**.

A set period of time corresponds to Daniel's prayer and fasting for twenty-one days while he waited for an answer to his prayer. During that time of prayer and fasting, he ate only foods from seed (some translations say vegetables).

The indefinite period of time is to live the Christian lifestyle in a post-Christian era. It is a choice to be transformed by the renewing of our mind that we may know God's perfect will and not be conformed to this world (Rom. 12:2). John defines this world as the lust of the flesh, the lust of the eyes, and the pride of life (1 John 2:15–17). It was those same three that Satan used to tempt Eve and was successful (Gen. 3:1–6). When he used the same three to try and tempt Jesus, he wasn't successful (Matt. 4:1–11).

By overcoming Satan's temptation, Jesus taught us that if we know God's commandments and delight in them, we will overcome Satan's temptations. That is why the Great Commission is so important—makes disciples (Matt. 28:18–20). Knowing the commandments and obeying them is living by faith (Rom. 1:17). It is allowing the transforming work of the Holy Spirit to be a witness to those who are not Christians. It isn't for a set period of time but until the Lord Jesus Christ returns in power and glory. It is **24/7/365**.

Paul's letter to the Ephesians exhorting them to put on the whole armor of God is the New Testament equivalent of the **Daniel Fast 24/7/365**. The whole armor of God enables the Christian to stand against the wiles of the devil, against the rulers of the darkness of this age, against spiritual hosts of wickedness in the heavenly places, and to stand in the evil day (Eph. 6:10–13).

Look at the words that make up the armor: truth, righteousness, peace, faith, salvation, and the word of God. The whole armor of God is being a Christian. Paul uses the phrase "put on" to tell his readers to live what they have already received. It had been given to them when they believed on the Lord Jesus Christ and were justified. He was saying the same thing when he wrote, "Put on the Lord Jesus Christ" (Rom. 13:14). They had already put on the Lord Jesus Christ when they were baptized (Gal. 3:27).

To the church at Rome, he also wrote, "Put on the weapon of light" (Rom. 13:12). To the Colossians, he wrote, "Put on therefore, as the elect of God, holy and beloved, bowels of mercies, kindness, humbleness of mind, meekness, longsuffering" (Col. 3:12).

In his second letter, Peter uses the phrases "add to," which corresponds to Paul's phrase "put on." Faith accepts Jesus Christ as Savor and Lord. It is essential; we can't be a Christian without faith. It is by faith that we are justified, born again, and become a new creation in Christ. But the Christian life is more than trusting and receiving; it is living what we have received by faith. That is why the exhortation, "add to" your faith.

We have already received by faith in Christ all things that pertain to life and godliness as well as exceeding great and precious promises (2 Peter 1:3, 4). They are already ours. Then in 2 Peter 1:5–7, Peter tells us to "add to" faith that received all things that pertain to life and godliness and the exceeding great and precious promise: virtue, knowledge, self-control, perseverance, godliness, kindness, and love (2 Peter 1:5–7 NKJV). Like Paul, he was saying live what you have received (verses 3, 4).

Peter concluded his exhortation by writing, "Therefore, brethren, be even more diligent to make your call and election sure, for if you do these things you will never stumble; for so an entrance will be supplied to you abundantly into the everlasting kingdom of our Lord and Savior Jesus Christ" (2 Peter 1:10, 11 NKJV). Look again at those two verses. In them, Peter sets forth the Christian lifestyle from the beginning until we enter the everlasting kingdom of our Lord and Savior Jesus Christ—the **Daniel Fast—24/7/365.**

Another example of the **Daniel Fast—24/7/365** in the New Testament is 1 Thessalonians 5:14–24 NKJV. In the verses, Paul explains how we are to live until the Lord returns: "Now we exhort you, brethren, warn those who are unruly, comfort the fainthearted, uphold the weak, be patient with all. See that no one renders evil for evil to anyone, but always pursue what is good both for yourselves and for all. Rejoice always, pray without ceasing, in everything give thanks; for this is the will of God in Christ Jesus for you. Do not quench the Spirit. Do not despise prophecies. Test all things; hold fast what is good. Abstain from every form of evil. Now may the God of peace himself sanctify you completely; and may your whole spirit, soul, and body be preserved blameless at the coming of our Lord Jesus Christ. He who calls you is faithful, who also will do it."

It is important to keep in mind that the **Daniel Fast** for an indefinite period of time isn't just to avoid being conformed to the non-Christian lifestyle, but also to receive wisdom from the Lord in order to minister to others as Daniel did in Babylon. The Lord used him greatly. He didn't criticize the king and the people but lived a godly lifestyle in their midst. He brought light into darkness. By Daniel being faithful to the king and the Lord, the king discovered the Lord God of Israel. Daniel fulfilled his role as a priest while living in the kingdom of Babylon (Ex. 19:5, 6). Christians are to do the same (1 Peter 2:9).

Daniel set a standard for both Jews and Christians—be people who delight in the Lord's commandments. One day I was driving down the interstate thinking about all the things that were wrong, and the thought came to me, "Stop looking at all that is wrong, and start doing what is right!" If all we do is avoid being conformed to the society, we will fail to be a Christian.

It isn't enough to look at what is wrong, listen to people talk about what is wrong, and be against it. Jesus went to that which was wrong and ministered. The apostles and disciples did the same following the day of Pentecost, and that is what Paul did after he was converted. Christians are called to do likewise. It isn't enough to criticize those who aren't Christians for not living the Christian lifestyle. They can't without being born again. It is only when the Christians live the lifestyle that is the result of the new birth that those who aren't Christians can see the alternative. The **Daniel Fast—24/7/365** is being an ambassador for Christ and a minister of reconciliation in the evil day (2 Cor. 5:18–20).

Twenty-One Days

Four years ago my wife and I were listening to three pastors discussing a twenty-one day fast on the Trinity Broadcasting Network. The discussion included both the **Traditional Fast** and the **Daniel Fast**. During the discussion, they talked about the number of Christians who were fasting twenty-one days in January that year and how the number of people fasting had grown over the past year. As I listened to the discussion, I knew that was something I wanted to do, and during the program, my wife came to the same conclusion.

After the program, my wife and I decided to do a combination of the **Traditional Fast** and the **Daniel Fast** for twenty-one days. We kept the Traditional Fast one day weekly as well as fasting lunch each of the twenty-one days. We made the decision not to eat any snacks, deserts, meat, poultry or dairy products, only foods from seeds for breakfast and dinner—fruits vegetables, nuts, and grains (Gen. 1:29).

We discovered that the **Daniel Fast,** three weeks in January, is time to wait in the Lord's presence and receive cleansing of our heart, revelation of Scripture, and instructions for the coming year or years. We decided to also include along with the **Daniel Fast— Twenty-One Days,** the **Daniel Fast—24/7/365,** and the **Chosen Fast—24/7/365**. More will be said about the **Chosen Fast** in the next chapter.

Practicing the Daniel Fast twenty-one days, the Traditional Fast weekly, the Daniel Fast—24/7/365, and the Chosen Fast—24/7/365 is time in the Lord's presence, and in his presence is fullness of joy (Psalm 16:11). Our mind is upon him, and he keeps us in perfect peace [shalom—see Chosen Fast—Promise] (Isaiah 26:3). We are waiting upon him and our strength is renewed (Isaiah 40:31). Consider for a moment those benefits. Each January, I experience joy, peace, strength, success, and a good life. But that is only starting the year. Those same benefits continue throughout the year as we practice the Chosen Fast—24/7/365, the Daniel Fast—24/7/365 and the Traditional Fast weekly.

Our motive for fasting isn't to receive the blessings, but rather be available to do whatever the Lord calls us to do. It is the covenant relationship—**Wisdom** (faithfulness to the Lord's commandments and faith in the Lord's faithfulness) **+ Promise** (the Lord's faithfulness to do what he said he would do). It is the kingdom of heaven (Matt. 5:3).

Chapter 4
The Chosen Fast

Instructions for fasting in the Old Testament are called the fast chosen by the Lord—the **Chosen Fast** (Isaiah 58:6–14). The instructions are practical ways of delighting in the Two Great Commandments—**Love the LORD** and **Love the Neighbor** (Deut. 6:5; Lev. 19:18; Matt. 22:37–40).

While there is no mention of the Chosen Fast in the New Testament, much of the teaching in the Gospels and Epistles are instructions for practicing the Chosen Fast. For example, the Sermon on the Mount contains virtues and commandments for practicing the Chosen Fast: poor in spirit, meekness, hungering and thirsting after righteousness, merciful, pure in heart, peacemakers, love your enemy, seek first the kingdom of God and his righteousness, do to others whatever you want them to do to you . "Not everyone who says to Me, 'Lord, Lord,' shall enter into the kingdom of heaven, but he who does the will of My Father in heaven" (Matt. 7:21 NKJV).

The Chosen Fast goes beyond the Traditional Fast—from a set period of time to 24/7/365, from sacrificing food to money, time, pleasure, and leisure, and from our needs to the needs of others. It is an entirely different way of living. It is the kingdom of God (Rom. 14:17), "Thy will be done on earth as it is in heaven." It is putting on Christ (Luke 4:18, 19), crucifying the flesh with its passions and desires (Gal. 5:24), living by faith (Rom. 1:17), building our house upon the rock (Matt. 7:24–27). It is the Lord Jesus Christ building his church and the gates of hell not prevailing against it (Matt. 16:16–19).

The **Chosen Fast** is comprised of three functions: (1) **Love the Neighbor:** Isaiah 58:6–7, 9b–10a, (2) **Promises:** 8–9a, 10b–12, and (3) **Love the LORD:** 13–14. The **Chosen Fast—Love the Neighbor, Promises,** and **Love the LORD**—is a microcosm of the Old Testament Covenant the Lord made with Israel at Mount Sinai. A covenant is an agreement between the Lord and his people in which he promises to do certain things and asks them to do certain things. It is an unequal covenant. What the people are asked to do is negligible in comparison to what the Lord promises to do. Rather than **2 + 2 = 4** which would be an equal covenant, it is **1 + 6 = 7.** I chose "**7**" because it is an expression of completeness in both the Old and the New Testaments.

Faithfulness to the covenant is to obey his commandments (Psalm 103:17, 18), and faithfulness to his commandments is **Wisdom.** The Lord's faithfulness to the covenant is to provide the **Promise.** In the **Chosen Fast, Love the neighbor,** and **Love the Lord** are faithfulness to the Lord's commandments—**Wisdom**. The Lord's faithfulness to his word is **Promise. Wisdom + Promise = Covenant, 1 + 6 = 7.** Faith in the Lord's faithfulness to give us the **Promise** without our being faithful to his commandments isn't **Covenant**. It is **Promise** ≠ **Covenant, 6 ≠ 7.**[3]

Wisdom is obeying the commandments, and the **Promises** are the life that emanates from **Wisdom**: living in the kingdom of God—righteousness, peace, and joy in the Holy Spirit (Rom. 14:17); living in the marvelous light—a priest (1 Peter 2:9); a branch in the vine—a disciple bearing much fruit (John 15:5), the new creation in Christ—a minister of reconciliation and an ambassador for Christ (2 Cor. 5:17–19).

The commandments are God's instructions for living in his kingdom. When we live in his kingdom, he lives in us (John 14:21, 23). Our fellowship is with the Father and his Son Jesus Christ (1 John 1:3).

Promises aren't received by asking the Lord for them, trusting him to give them, or confessing them. They are the life that comes from obeying his commandments—the covenant relationship. We don't go to the Bible and look up a certain promise, see what the commandment is to receive it, and then obey the commandment in order to receive the promise. Rather **Wisdom** and **Promises** are a daily lifestyle. As we obey the commandments, the promises we need are given to us (Isaiah 58:6–14; Matt. 6:33; Phil. 4:19). The combination is fellowship with God, giving and receiving grace.

Foolishness is disobeying the commandments, and the curse is death that comes from foolishness: the wages of sin is death (Rom. 6:23), no inheritance in the kingdom of God (Gal. 5:19–21), and living in the darkness (1 Peter 2:9).

Love the Neighbor

(1)   Isaiah 58:6–7, 9b–10:

6 Is not this the fast that I have chosen? To lose the bands of wickedness, to undo the heavy burdens, and to let the oppressed go free, and that ye break every yoke?

7 Is it not to deal thy bread to the hungry, and that thou bring the poor that are cast out to thy house? When thou seest the naked, that thou cover him; and that thou hide not thyself from thine own flesh?

9b If thou take away from the midst of thee the yoke, the putting forth of the finger, and speaking vanity;

10 And if thou draw out thy soul to the hungry, and satisfy the afflicted soul.

Love the Neighbor comes before **Love the Lord** in the **Chosen Fast,** which is the opposite of the way it is written other places in the Bible—**Love the Lord** first then **Love the Neighbor.** However, both the Old and New Testaments remind us that what we do to others we do to the Lord. When David committed adultery with Bathsheba, the wife of Uriah, and was responsible for Uriah's death, he repented of his sins and acknowledged that what he had done to them was sins against the Lord. "Against thee, thee only, have I sinned, and done this evil in your sight" (Psalm 51:4a). When Saul was converted on the road to Damascus, he heard a voice saying to him, "Saul, Saul, why persecutest thou me?" He was persecuting Christians, but in so doing, he was persecuting Christ (Acts 9:4).

To love the Lord is to keep his commandments (Deut. 30:15, 16, 20; John 14:15). Keeping his commandments is wisdom (Deut. 4:5, 6; Matt. 7:24–27). Wisdom is to love our neighbor as ourselves (Lev. 19:18). Since what we do to others, we do to the Lord, when we love our neighbor, we love the Lord—the Two Great Commandments (Matt. 22:37–39).

Jesus summarized all the Law and the Prophets in the Two Great Commandments (Matt. 22:37–39). The person who delights in the Two Great Commandments fulfills the Law (the first five books of the Bible) and the Prophets. Both the "Don't" and the "Do" in the Law and the Prophets are fulfilled. Obeying the "Don't" in the Law and the Prophets is not the end. It keeps us from dying. "The wages of sin is death" (Rom. 6:23). But obeying the "Do," **Love the Lord and Neighbor,** is life.

The ministry of the righteous at the time when the Son of Man comes in his glory (Matthew 25:35–36) is very similar to **Love the Neighbor** in Isaiah 58:7. They feed the hungry, give water to the thirsty, care for the strangers, provide clothing for the naked, and visit the sick and those in prison. The King will answer and say to them, "Verily I say unto you, Inasmuch as ye have done it to one of the least of these my brethren, ye have done it unto me." By fulfilling the **Second Great Commandment**, "Thou shalt love thy neighbor as thy self," (Matt. 22:39), they fulfilled the **First Great Commandment**, "Thou shalt love the Lord thy God with all thy heart and all they soul and all thy strength" (Matt.22:37).

On the other hand, those who didn't minister to the hungry, thirsty, naked, sick, and prisoners didn't minister to the Lord. Jesus' teaching in those verses of

Scripture gives us insight into the relationship between the Chosen Fast and righteousness, eternal life, and the kingdom of God. The setting of Matthew 25:35, 36 is the Second Coming of Christ, which means those who enter into the kingdom of God when he returns will be practicing the Chosen Fast.

Love the Neighbor includes the enemy. Jesus said, "You have heard that it was said, 'You shall love your neighbor and hate your enemy.' But I say to you, love your enemies, bless those who curse you, do good to those who hate you, and pray for those who spitefully use you and persecute you'" (Matt.5:43, 44 NKJV).

Jesus gave the parable of the Good Samaritan (Luke 10:30–5) in answer to the question, "Who is my neighbor?" The Samaritan was on a journey when he came upon a man who had been beaten, robbed, and left half dead. The victim was a Jew, and the Jews hated the Samaritans. The Samaritan obeyed the commandment of Jesus (Matt. 5:43, 44). He loved his neighbor who was his enemy.

He bound up the man's wounds, poured in oil and wine, placed him on his own mount, took him to an inn, asked the innkeeper to care for the man, paid the innkeeper, and said if additional money was needed, he would pay it when he returned. He practiced the Chosen Fast. The man who asked the question, "Who is my neighbor?" also asked, "What shall I do to inherit eternal life?" After giving the parable, Jesus gave him the answer, "Go and do likewise." Practicing the Chosen Fast isn't doing good works to earn eternal life—practicing the Chosen Fast is eternal life.

Jonah's response to the enemy was just the opposite of the Good Samaritan. He didn't want to preach to the people of Nineveh; they were his enemies. He wanted them punished, not forgiven. We each are confronted with similar circumstances as the Good Samaritan and Jonah. Will we act like Jonah or the Good Samaritan? We can act like Jonah and desire their punishment, and be swallowed by a whale. Or, we can act like the Good Samaritan, leave our prejudices, fortresses, and barriers, and cross over into the enemies' prejudices, fortresses, and barriers, and minister to the person in need, and **live**. The choice we make is to **live** or to **die**.

Paul explained going beyond "Don't" to "Do" in his letter to the Christians in Rome. "Owe no man anything, but to love one another: for he that loveth another hath fulfilled the law. For this, Thou shalt not commit adultery, Thou shalt not kill, Thou shalt not steal, Thou shalt not bear false witness, Thou shalt not covet; and if there be any other commandment, it is briefly comprehended in this saying, namely, Thou shalt love thy neighbour as thyself. Love worketh no ill to his neighbour: therefore love is the fulfilling of the law" (Rom. 13:8–10).

Both the new birth and the Holy Spirit are essential for practicing the Chosen Fast. The new birth includes receiving the Holy Spirit, and it is the Holy Spirit who produces fruit in our life: love, joy, peace, patience, kindness, goodness, faithfulness, gentleness and self-control (Gal. 5:22, 23 NIV). In 1 Cor. 13:4, 5, Paul contrasts the fruit of the Spirit—love for the neighbor—with works of the flesh (Gal. 5:19, 21), which harm the neighbor. Love for the neighbor is patient and kind. But envy, boasting, pride, rudeness, self-seeking, being easily angered and keeping a record of wrongs harms the neighbor. The person who harms the neighbor doesn't love the Lord. To love the neighbor is life, and to harm the neighbor is death.

The ministries in Isaiah 58: 6, 7, 9b, and 10 require God's love, the love that gives. To love the neighbor is to give sacrificially to the neighbor. God's love gives. "For God so loved the world that He gave His only begotten Son, that whosoever believeth in him should not perish, but have everlasting life" (John 3:16). When we believe in his Son, we are born again (John 3:5–8); we become children of God. He is our Father. He gives us his Spirit—the Holy Spirit—who pours God's love into our heart (Rom. 5:5).

John 3:16 is twofold: we receive God's love, which saves us (John 3:16), and then others receive God's love through us to save them. That is the ministry of reconciliation. God's work through Christ to save us is given to us through Christ in us in order to save others: "Now all things are of God, who has reconciled us to Himself through Jesus Christ, and has given us the ministry of reconciliation, that is, that God was in Christ reconciling the world to Himself, not imputing their trespasses to them, and has committed to us the word of reconciliation" (2 Cor. 5:18, 19 NKJV).

Love is the fruit of the Spirit, and giving is a gift of the Spirit (Rom. 12:8). The Chosen Fast requires both fruit and gifts of the Spirit. In addition to the gift of giving, other gifts necessary to practice the Chosen Fast are ministry, exhortation, showing mercy (Rom. 12:7, 8); word of wisdom, word of knowledge, faith, healings, miracles, and helps (1 Cor. 13:8–10, 28).

God loves a cheerful giver. We give, and God is able to make all grace abound toward us that we, always having all sufficiency in all things, may have an abundance for every good work (2 Cor. 9:8 NKJV). Those who are righteous give, and there is no end to giving because God never lacks resources. It is like the widow who gave Elijah the last food she had, and the Lord replaced it. So she, her son, and Elijah continued to eat from it for a year (1 Kings 17:8–16). Even though we give what looks to be the last we have, we can give joyfully knowing we can never give it all. The Lord will supply (2 Cor. 9:8).

Love that gives is righteousness (Psalm 37:21, 112:9). Righteousness is life—eternal life, the life of God. The just (the righteous) shall live by faith (Rom. 1:17; Hab. 2:4). To live by faith is wisdom—faith in God's faithfulness and faithfulness to his commandments. The person who receives God's love that gives doesn't love the neighbor to receive eternal life; but because he has eternal life, he has love that gives. We are his children, and faithfulness is a characteristic of our Father just as love and giving are characteristics. All three: faithfulness, love, and giving, come from the Spirit of God dwelling in us and bearing witness that we are the children of God (Rom. 8:16).

Promises

(2)   Isaiah 58:8–10b, 11–12, 14b:

8 Then shall thy light break forth as the morning, and thine health shall spring forth speedily: and thy righteousness shall go before thee; the glory of the LORD shall be thy rereward.

9 Then shalt thou call, and the LORD shall answer; thou shalt cry, and he shall say, Here I am.

10b...then shall thy light rise in obscurity, and thy darkness be as the noon day:

11 And the LORD shall guide thee continually, and satisfy thy soul in drought, and make fat thy bones: and thou shalt be like a watered garden, and like a spring of water, whose waters fail not.

12 And they that shall be of thee shall build the old waste places: thou shalt raise up the foundations of many generations; and thou shalt be called, The repairer of the breach, The restorer of paths to dwell in.

14b and I will cause thee to ride upon the high places of the earth, and feed thee with the heritage of Jacob thy father: for the mouth of the Lord hath spoken it.

The Promises in the Chosen Fast are health, righteousness, protection, answered prayer, guidance, and success—*shalom*. *Shalom* is a Hebrew word that is translated "peace" in our English Bible, but it is far more than tranquility or the absence of war. It includes all the promises in the Chosen Fast. Therefore, if we practice the Chosen Fast, we don't have to ask for the promises. Rather we can thank him for them, which is the will of God in Christ Jesus (1 Thess. 5:18).

We don't have to worry about our health, our prayers being answered, protection, guidance, and success; we can rejoice (Phil. 4:4, 6). We don't have to fear when bad news comes. Our heart is steadfast, trusting in the Lord (Psalm 112:7). We give the Lord thanks for his protection and continue to practice the Chosen Fast in the midst of the bad news. We don't have to practice the Traditional Fast to receive protection, guidance, healing, or answered prayers, which are Chosen Fast promises.

Consider the similarities between love for the neighbor and promises in the Chosen Fast and love for the neighbor and promises in Psalms and Proverbs: "He who gives to the poor will not lack" (Proverbs 28:27 NKJV). "Blessed is he that considereth the poor: the LORD will deliver him in time of trouble. The LORD will preserve him, and keep him alive; and he shall be blessed upon the earth: and thou wilt not deliver him unto the will of his enemies. The LORD will strengthen him upon the bed of languishing: thou wilt make all his bed in his sickness" (Psalm 41:1–3). We also find the same similarities in the New Testament—the Chosen Fast is seeking first the kingdom of God and his righteousness, and our needs will be provided (Matt. 6:33; Phil. 4:19).

Love the Lord

> (3)   Isaiah 58:13–14:
> *13 If thou turn away thy foot from the Sabbath,*
> *from doing thy pleasure on my holy day; and call*
> *the Sabbath a delight, the holy of the LORD,*
> *honourable; and shalt honour him, not doing thine*

own ways, nor finding thine own pleasure, nor
speaking thine own words:
14 Then shalt thou delight thyself in the LORD.

We love the Lord by keeping his commandments:

That thou mayest love the LORD thy God, and that
thou mayest obey His voice, and that thou mayest cling unto
him: for he is thy life, and the length of thy days: that thou
mayest dwell in the land which the LORD sware unto thy
fathers, to Abraham, to Isaac, and to Jacob, to give them
(Deut. 30:20).

If ye love me, keep my commandments (John 14:15).

For this is the love of God that we keep his command-
ments (1 John 5:3a).

Whoso keepeth his word, in him verily is the love of
God perfected: hereby know we that we are in him (1 John
2:5).

If ye keep my commandments, ye shall abide in my
love; even as I have kept my Father's commandments, and
abide in his love (John 15:10).

The Greek New Testament from which our English Bible was translated has two different words that
have been translated "love" in our English Bible:

1.   Αγάπάω [ag-ap-ah-o]: **God's love**
2.   Φιλεω [fil-eh-o]: **friendship love, family love**

Since both are translated "love" in the English lan-
guage, the commandment to love God and neighbor gets
confused with friendship love or family love. Friendship
love or family love is reciprocal. It must receive love in
order to give love. Without receiving love, there is a

limited amount of love to give. If any imbalance goes on very long, there will probably be a breakup of the family or friendship. God's love doesn't require reciprocity—receiving love in order to give love. Therefore, God's love takes over when friendship love and family love fail. It continues to love the person who doesn't reciprocate. It is the person who has God's love that can love the neighbor who is an enemy.

Friendship or family love is natural, but God's love is supernatural. It is poured into our heart by the Holy Spirit when we are justified (Rom. 5:5). Love for the neighbor, God's love, transcends friendship and family love; it is sacrificial love. It gives and forgives. It is the character of God. God's love was demonstrated when he gave his Son to die for us while we were yet sinners. Jesus demonstrated God's love when he forgave the people who crucified him. Like his Lord, Steven, a man full of the Holy Spirit and faith, forgave his executioners who were stoning him to death (Acts 7:60).

God is love, and to be filled with the Holy Spirit is to be filled with God's love. It is God's love that motivates us to minister to others the gifts the Holy Spirit gives to us: helping, serving, encouraging, and bearing one another's burdens—the Chosen Fast. With few exceptions, when you see "love" in the New Testament, it is God's love—Ἀγάπη. Another Greek word translated love in English, Ἐρός [er-os], sensual love, isn't found in the New Testament, but its works are: "sexual immorality, impurity and debauchery...." (Gal. 5:19 NIV) Ἀγάπη is life, and Ἐρός is death.

To love the Lord is to delight in his commandments, and delighting in his commandments is delighting in the Lord (Isaiah 58:13, 14). Delighting in the commandment takes priority over our pleasure, our ways. It is delighting in the Lord, and we have the true desires of our heart (Psalm 37:4): (1) wisdom which makes it possible (2) to obey the Second Great Commandment—**Love the Neighbor**—which in turn makes it possible (3) to obey the First Great Commandment—**Love the LORD** with all our heart.

When we have the desires of our heart, we experience the words of Jesus: "At that day ye shall know that I am in my Father, and ye in me, and I in you" (John 14:20). That is oneness with God, and there is nothing in this life that compares to that; it is experiencing the life of the age to come now.

Keeping the Sabbath holy is one of the Ten Commandments (Ex. 20:8–1), but it is also the sign of the Mosaic Covenant (Ex. 31:13). Therefore the instructions for keeping the Sabbath, delighting in the commandment, and delighting in the Lord are standards for delighting in all the commandments and delighting in the Lord. Isaiah 58:13 helps us to understand the difference between obeying the commandment and delighting in it. We may obey the commandment out of fear of the consequence of disobeying and not honor the commandment or the Lord. We may also obey while at the same time resenting the commandment and be angry at the Lord for giving it to us.

We delight in the commandment and honor it when we understand its value for us as well as for others. That was true in the Old Testament as well as in the New. It is given to us by our heavenly Father who loves us and knows what is the very best for us. It is out of that understanding that we delight in the commandment and in the Lord. We honor the commandment, and we honor the Lord.

Wisdom—obeying the Great Commandments— is the desire of the heart of the wise, and it is received by the righteous that delight in the Lord (Psalm 37:4). Wisdom is more precious than rubies, and all the things you may desire cannot compare with her. Length of days, riches and honor, ways of pleasantness, paths of peace, tree of life, and happiness are promises that go with wisdom (Proverbs 3:16–18); but they are not the heart's desires of the wise. Why? We can't delight in the Lord if our desires are his promises. We delight in him when our desires are to love him with all our heart and our neighbor as ourselves. We are seeking first the kingdom of God and his righteousness, and the promises will be added to us (Matt. 6:33).

I was saved at a tent revival on a Thursday evening in August of 1958. I was twenty-four years old. The following Sunday morning, my wife and I took our two daughters, one two years old and the other three months old, and went to Sunday school and morning worship service. I had attended Sunday school a few times in my life, but I had only attended a Sunday morning worship service one time that I can remember, and that was to recognize the Boy Scout troop of which I was a member at the church that sponsored the troop.

Until that morning, when we got up earlier than usual on Sunday morning to go to Sunday school and morning worship service, I thought I had to sleep in on Sunday morning or I wouldn't make it through the next week. But when we arrived home from church that Sunday, I realized that I was refreshed in a way that I had never been refreshed in my life. I was far more refreshed than when I slept in on Sunday morning. I experienced the Sabbath rest (Heb. 4:3–11).

Before that Sunday, not only did I sleep in on Sunday morning, but I went to bed early on Sunday evening in order to be rested for Monday to start the work week. But that first Sunday that I went to Sunday school and morning worship service, I was so refreshed that I went to the Sunday evening service. After getting up early and staying up later than usual on Sunday evening, I was more rested and refreshed on Monday morning than I had ever been.

At that time, I was working three shifts. When I worked day shift, I missed Sunday school and morning worship service. When I worked the afternoon shift, I missed the Sunday evening service. On the midnight shift, I missed Sunday school and morning worship service. Being absent from the Sunday services deprived me of the Sabbath rest. As soon as an all day-shift job, 8:00–4:30, Monday through Friday, was available, I bid on it so that I could be off every Sunday. It was a pay cut, but pay did not compensate for the spiritual and physical refreshing I received from the Sabbath rest.

That was fifty-two years ago, and I have never found anything as refreshing and restful as the Sabbath rest, being in worship service with other believers honoring the Lord. I delight in the Lord's Day. I don't observe it out of law but grace. It is for my benefit. I understand the Lord's words, "The Sabbath was made for man, and not man for the Sabbath" (Mark 2:27). I denied myself some money that I could have used to buy things or for pleasure, but things and pleasure cannot compare to what I received in return. I received life.

Every day, not just Sunday, is the Lord's Day when we practice the Chosen Fast. Every day is the day the Lord has made, and I will rejoice and be glad in it (Psalm 118:24). However that doesn't replace the Sabbath day to assemble with other believers, minister to one another, and minister to the Lord—the Chosen Fast. For the greater majority of Christians, Sunday has been and is the Sabbath. It is the time for the assembly of the church on earth and the church in heaven (Heb. 12:22–24). It is a time of fellowship, χοινωνια [koy-nohn-ee-ah], giving and receiving grace. It has benefits that can't be received in any other way.

Worship on the Sabbath is far more than singing choruses, praying, and listening to the message by the pastor. It is fellowship with one another before, after, and during the time together. It is greeting one another, getting acquainted with one another, praying for one another, encouraging one another, etc. It is the Chosen Fast. Worship directed to the Lord without fellowship with one another is not fellowship with the Lord. If worship is directed to the Lord only, there is no need to assemble together. We can worship at home, but that

wouldn't be the Chosen Fast. It wouldn't be χοινωνια—
giving and receiving grace—gifts of the Spirit.

If I am not in fellowship with other believers because of what someone said or did to me, I am without
God's love. I had friendship love, and when I didn't receive love, I didn't have any love to give. I am keeping a
record of wrongs. I am not a minister of reconciliation.
I don't love my enemies. I don't love the Lord because I
don't love my neighbor. I am not practicing the Chosen
Fast. I have forfeited the Promises of the Chosen Fast.

So important was the assembly of the believers
and the fellowship of the Holy Spirit that Paul wouldn't
allow those who sinned and wouldn't repent to be par-
takers of the fellowship. They were then defenseless
against Satan who could destroy their life, and in so doing, Paul's prayer was that they might repent (I Cor.
5:1–5; I Tim.1:20).

Not only is every day the Lord's Day when practicing the Chosen Fast, but every day is worship in spirit and truth as well (John 4:23–24). God is Spirit, and
in order to worship him in spirit, we must receive his
Spirit, the Holy Spirit. The only way we can receive his
Spirit is by repenting of our sins and believing on his Son
Jesus Christ (Rom. 5:1–5).

At the time we receive the Holy Spirit, Jesus, the
great high priest, washes the true worshipers from their
sins in his own blood and makes them a kingdom and
priests to serve his God and Father (Rev. 1:5, 6 NIV).
Their bodies become temples of the Holy Spirit (I Cor.
6:19). Unlike the Old Testament priests who offered
animals as substitutes for their sins, New Testament

priests offer their bodies as living sacrifices to God, which is their spiritual worship (Rom. 12:1 RSV).

The tabernacle in the wilderness was a dwelling place of God among his people. It was a type of heaven. God was present in the cloud, the Shekinah glory. Jesus replaced the tabernacle and temple in the Old Testament (John 1:14) as well as the high priest and the sacrifices he offered for sin (Heb. 9:11, 12). Jesus became the mercy seat and the atoning sacrifice. The Holy of Holies was brought out from behind the curtain and made visible to all through Jesus on the cross (Rom. 3:25).

Propitiation is the translation of the Greek New Testament word, ἱλαστήριον [hil-as-tay-ree-on] in the KJV and NKJV. It is translated sacrifice of atonement in the NIV and mercy seat in Hebrews 9:5 KJV and NKJV. The Septuagint, the Greek translation of the Hebrew Old Testament, translates ἱλαστήριον as mercy in the phrase mercy seat in Exodus 25:17. Jesus is the great high priest, and we are priests.

Old Testament Most Holy Place
> Located in the Tabernacle or Temple
> A dwelling place of God
> Entered once a year by the high priest
> Mercy seat—gold
> Atoning Sacrifice—blood of sacrificed animal
> Offered by the high priest
> Yearly on the Day of Atonement

New Testament Most Holy Place
> Located in the believer's heart
> A dwelling place of God

The spirit of the believer dwells there continually
Jesus—High Priest
Jesus—Atoning Sacrifice
Jesus—Mercy Seat

In the Old Testament, God entered the Most Holy Place, and the high priest met him there once a year on the Day of Atonement. But in the New Testament, Jesus the High Priest, Mercy Seat, Atoning Sacrifice, enters into the heart of the priest and dwells there—the Most Holy Place—Christ in us.

Jesus said, "In My father's house are many mansions; if it were not so, I would have told you. I go to prepare a place for you, And if I go and prepare a place for you, I will come again and receive you to Myself; that where I am, there you may be also" (John 14:2, 3 NKJV). Then he said, "If anyone loves Me, he will keep My word; and My Father will love him, and We will come to him and make our home with him" (John 14:23 NKJV). The same Greek word, μονή [mon-ay], that is translated mansions in John 14:2 is translated home in John 14:23 NKJV. The Most Holy Place in the New Testament is the home that God makes in the heart of the priest. The spirit of the priest dwells in the home with God. That was true of the Old Testament temple as well. David wrote, "We shall be satisfied with the goodness of Your house, of Your holy temple" (Psalm 65:4 NKJV).

Our spirit living in the home God the Father and Son make with us is experiencing something of what it will be like living in the place he has gone to prepare for us. Paul wasn't with the apostles when Jesus gave the teaching on making his home with us and preparing a place for us in the future. So from the revelation he received from the Lord after his conversion, Paul calls the home the Lord makes with us here and now the heavenly places in Christ (Eph. 1:3; 2:6, 7).

The spirit of the priest in fellowship with the High Priest experiences eternal life, the resurrection, and the kingdom of God, which is both the first fruits and the guarantee of the full inheritance (Eph. 1:13, 14). The Eternal enters the temporal, and Immortality enters mortality. God the Father, Son, and Holy Spirit are in fellowship with the spirit of the priest. At death the procedure is reversed—the spirit of the priest leaves the temporal and enters the eternal. Mortality enters into immortality. The body returns to dust and is resurrected at the First Resurrection.

Daily I take time to meditate upon my spirit worshiping in the Most Holy Place in the presence of the resurrected Christ, the Holy Spirit changing my spirit into the image of Christ (2 Cor. 3:18), and the power of Christ in me—all authority in heaven and earth (Matt. 28:18–20). I experienced the Eternal in the temporal—the first fruits of the age to come.

That which takes place inwardly in the Most Holy Place of the heart of the priest also takes place outwardly in the worship service with other believers (Heb. 12:22–24). In the worship service, the Eternal enters the temporal and the Immortal enters the mortal, and for that brief time of worship the temporal enters into the Eternal, and the mortal enters the Immortal. Worship with other priests keeps us from being swallowed up by the temporal and losing sight of the Eternal. We can better appreciate the warning—not forsaking the assembling of ourselves together with other priests (Heb. 10:19–25).

Jesus said God's word is truth (John 17:17). That which takes place inwardly, in the heart, worship in spirit—Christ in us—takes place outwardly in the body which is worship in truth—in Christ. It is the new creation in Christ; the old has gone, the new has come (2 Cor. 5:17 NIV). It is putting off the old man and putting on the new man. It is crucifying the flesh. It is being who we are in Christ. To worship in truth is to live the truth—wisdom. The worshiper's body offered as a living sacrifice to God and a spiritual mind make possible outwardly what is inwardly the kingdom of heaven (Matt. 5:3, 10).

Worship in truth is God doing his work through the worshiper. God was in Christ reconciling the world to himself, and has given to the priest the ministry of reconciliation (2 Cor. 5:18). It is called the Great Commission (Matt. 28:18–20). The spirit of the priest in fellowship with the High Priest receives from him wisdom from God—and righteousness and sanctification and redemption (1 Cor. 1:30). They are words that describe the new creation (2 Cor. 5:17) with the new heart and new spirit (Ezek. 36:26) that has been given a new commandment (John 13:34, 35) for the new covenant (Heb. 12:24).

The Hebrew word חסד [kheh-sed] is translated "mercy," "love," "steadfast love," and "loyalty" in our English Bible. The word is used several times in Psalm

136:1–24 where it is translated "mercy" in the KJV and NKJV, "love" in the NIV, and "steadfast love" in the RSV. It is the Lord's covenant love. That same covenant love is implanted in the spirit of the priest who is in fellowship with the High Priest in the Most Holy Place.

What I found true of delighting in the Sabbath and the benefits I receive, I find true of all the commandments. Delighting in them is a choice to live (Deut. 30:19, 20). They are life, God's grace, and the wisdom of God (Deut. 4:5, 6). Obeying them is wisdom (Matt. 7:24–27). I understand why nothing compares to wisdom (Proverbs 8:10, 11). It is fellowship with God (I John 1:3, 4); it is God dwelling in us (John 14:21; I John 3:24). We are one with God (John 14:20; 15:1–8).

It is only when I understand the love of God for me that I can delight in the commandments and delight in the LORD. The combination is called the fear of the LORD in the Old Testament. Some definitions for the fear of the LORD are "reverence, respect, awe," etc. While those definitions are true, the fear of the LORD is so much more. The best way to understand the meaning of the fear of the LORD is to read through Psalms and Proverbs and write down the verses that contain the phrase "fear of the LORD." After writing them down, study them carefully, and you will have a better understanding of the fear of the Lord. The following three verses contain the phrase "fear of the LORD."

Blessed is the man who fears the LORD,

Who delights greatly in His commandments (Psalm 112:2).

The fear of the LORD is the beginning of knowledge,

But fools despise wisdom and instruction (Proverbs 1:7).

The fear of the LORD is the beginning of wisdom,

And the knowledge of the Holy One is understanding (Proverbs 9:10).

Psalms and Proverbs are Hebrew poetry. Each of the above verses contains two sentences. In Psalm 112:2 and Proverbs 9:10, the second sentence repeats the thought in the first using different but similar meaning words. So, from Psalm 112:2 and Proverbs 9:10, we discover that the fear of the LORD is delighting greatly in his commandments (Psalm 112:2) and having knowledge of the Holy One (Proverbs 9:10).

Proverbs also contrasts the lifestyle of the wise and the foolish. Therefore the thought in the second sentence is just the opposite in meaning from the first. The person who fears the LORD desires wisdom and instruction and searches for it as hidden treasure, but the person who doesn't fear the Lord despises wisdom and instruction (Proverbs 1:7).

Following are some additional verses from Proverbs containing the phrase "fear of the LORD." As you meditate upon the verses, look for the relationship between the commandments and promises in them and the ones in the Chosen Fast. Keep in mind that the "fear of the LORD" is to delight in his commandments (I have inserted [delight in his commandments]):

Be not wise in thine own eyes: fear the LORD *[delight in his commandments], and depart from evil. It shall be health to thy navel, and marrow to thy bones* (Proverbs 3:7, 8).

The fear of the LORD [delight in his command-ments] *prolongeth days* (Proverbs 10:27).

In the fear of the LORD [delight in his command-ments] *is strong confidence: and his children shall have a place of refuge* (Proverbs 14:26).

The fear of the LORD [delight in his command-ments] *is a fountain of life, to depart from the snares of death* (Proverbs 14:27).

The fear of the LORD [delight in his command-ments] *tendeth to life: and he that hath it shall abide satisfied; he shall not be visited with evil* (Proverbs 19:23).

The fear of the LORD is the beginning of wisdom about God and his will (Proverbs 9:10). It is knowledge of God and us in the light of the revelation of God. The fear of the LORD brings about repentance—a change of mind, and a change in our values, way of thinking, and living. It is turning from being a fool to being wise, turning from a god we have conceived in our mind to God who reveals himself to us in the Scriptures, and turning from disobeying God's commandments to delighting in them (Psalm 37:4; Isaiah 58:13, 14).[4] It is following Christ and not Adam. Every Lord's Day is a reminder of the benefits of delighting in the commandments and practicing the Chosen Fast.

24/7/365

Ministries listed in the Chosen Fast are to loose the bonds of wickedness; to undo the heavy burdens; to let the oppressed go free; to break every yoke; to share your bread with the hungry, and to bring to your house the poor who are cast out; when you see the naked, to cover him, and not hide yourself from your own flesh; to take away the yoke from your midst, the pointing of the finger, and speaking wickedness; and to satisfy the afflicted soul (Isaiah 58:6, 7, 10a NKJV). These can't be confined to a certain day as the Traditional Fast. There is no way of predicting when the ministry will be needed. Therefore the **Chosen Fast** is **24/7/365**. It is renewing the covenant daily: **Wisdom + Promise = Covenant**.

The Good Samaritan practiced the Chosen Fast (Luke 10:30–35). His ministry didn't take place on a day he had set aside to fast and pray. Rather it was unexpected. He was on a journey and came upon the man who had been beaten, robbed, and left half dead. The Samaritan had places to go and things to do, but when he saw the man in need, he stopped and helped him. He bound up his wounds, poured in oil and wine, placed him on his own mount, took him to an inn, asked the inn keeper to care for him, paid the inn keeper, and said if additional money was needed, he would pay when he returned. He gave of his time, walked instead of riding, and gave money to care for the man that he could have used for himself.

People who have health problems such as diabetes shouldn't practice the Traditional Fast, going without food, without first consulting their physician, but they can practice the Chosen Fast. It doesn't require a person to go without food, but the self-sacrifice is as demanding if not more so than the Traditional Fast.

Steve is an electrical engineer at a chemical plant, plays the trumpet at each of the church services, and practices every Wednesday evening from 6:00–6:45 with the worship team. It is very seldom that Steve misses a service or practice. Not only is he involved in the music ministry, but he is also one of the church deacons. In addition to all of that, Steve and his wife Carrie host and teach a monthly home Bible study.

Carrie is the children's pastor, which includes children's church each Sunday morning from 10:45–12:00. She also plans the Easter egg hunt to reach children and families in the neighborhood. In order to promote the Easter egg hunt, she involves the church in our town's Easter parade. She also plans for the annual Vacation Bible School, the annual Fall Harvest Festival, and the Christmas program.

Before Carrie assumed the responsibility of children's pastor, their son James, who was born with Down syndrome, was diagnosed with leukemia. He was admitted to the children's hospital in Pittsburgh for treatment, which lasted several weeks. Shortly after James completed his treatments for leukemia, he was diagnosed with diabetes. His blood sugar level went so high that it was life threatening.

My wife and I went to Steve and Carrie's Bible study one Sunday evening. When we got there, Carrie was feeding James. Not only is James a diabetic, but he has a disorder that doesn't allow him to digest his food sufficiently; he also has a problem swallowing. Carrie prepared James a special diet of baby food—fruit and vegetables. In addition to the special diet, he is fed a liquid diet through a feeding tube into his stomach. After the Bible study, Steve prepared the liquid diet for the feeding tube, and using a syringe, he inserted the liquid into the feeding tube.

That morning Carrie had worked with the children during children's church in preparation for the Christmas play the following Sunday evening. After church, she worked with twelve others adults that she had asked to help her decorate the fellowship hall for the reception following the Christmas program. If that wasn't enough, she was scheduled for surgery on Tuesday for a biopsy on her thyroid. The biopsy revealed that there was no cancer, and the following Sunday she directed an entertaining Christmas play followed by a reception.

How many people can handle all of that? How many would have become angry at God and given up their faith? That evening at the Bible study, I witnessed the **Chosen Fast—24/7/365: Love the Neighbor, Promises,** and **Love the Lord**.

Not all 24/7/365 care-giving is the Chosen Fast, and both the caregiver and the one cared for miss the kingdom of God—righteousness and peace and joy in the Holy Spirit (Rom. 14:17). But the caregiver who practices the Chosen Fast is righteous and receives peace and joy as well as the one being cared for.

None of us know when we may be faced with a challenge that requires care-giving 24/7/365: an injury that leaves a child or spouse paralyzed, a terminal illness, a stroke, dementia, Alzheimer's, children born with Down syndrome, cerebral palsy, autism, etc. It happens every day for many people. There are those who don't accept the challenge, and there are those who reluctantly accept the challenge. They would rather not, but they feel they have no choice. Both the life of the caregiver and the one cared for suffer. Then there are those like Steve and Carrie who accept the challenge. They practice the **Chosen Fast—24/7/365,** and both the caregiver and the one cared for experience the kingdom of God.

My sisters Sharon and Mary care for our other sister Sheila, who has Alzheimer's. Sheila doesn't know any of us. She can walk and feed herself with assistance, but other than that, Mary and Sharon care for her 24/7/365. Their care for Sheila is the Chosen Fast. All three experience love, joy, and peace. Sheila has cancer as well as Alzheimer's. She has done remarkably well with both, and it is the result of the care she receives.

The care by Mary and Sharon for Sheila is an example of, "Blessed are the poor in spirit: for theirs is the kingdom of heaven" (Matt. 5:3). Poor in spirit is humble service to others. It is righteousness (Matt. 25: 36–40). It is washing the other person's feet. Washing other people's feet literally is symbolical of humble service to others, but the ritual is no substitute for humble service (John 13:13–17). The person who serves others is the greatest person in the kingdom of heaven (Matt. 23:11).

Chapter 5
The Chosen Fast and Prayer

The promises received by the person who practices the **Chosen Fast** are healing, righteousness, protection, answered prayer, guidance, and success. They are a summary of the benefits of the Pentateuch—*shalom* (see chapter on the **Chosen Fast** and **Promises**). The promises include the basic human needs. If we are practicing the Chosen Fast, we don't have to ask for the promises. Rather, we thank the Lord for them.

Asking the Lord for our needs reveals that we don't understand the covenant relationship—do what the Lord asks us to do, and he will do what he says he will do. "But my God shall supply all your need according to His riches in glory by Christ Jesus" (Phil. 4:19). Those words were written to Christians who had ministered to Paul's needs. They practiced the Chosen Fast. We can minister to other's needs knowing that the Lord will supply our needs. We can boldly say as David did, "The LORD is my Shepherd; I shall not want" (Psalm 23:1). When a need or a crisis arises in our life, instead of asking, we can give thanks to the Lord for his faithfulness to his word.

Practicing the Chosen Fast enables us to change the focus from ourselves to others. Asking rather than giving thanks may not only reveal a lack of understanding of the covenant relationship but a lack of understanding of who the God of the Bible is. In the New Testament, Christians are called children, slaves, and sheep. Children don't tell the parents what to do; the parents tell the children what to do. Slaves don't tell their master what to do; the master tells the slaves what to do. Sheep don't tell the shepherd what to do; they listen to the voice of the shepherd (John 10:27). How easily we can reverse the roles. Instead of listening and obeying what the Lord tells us to do, we tell him what we want him to do for us as well as for others.

God was known in the Old Testament as both **LORD** and **Lord**. "O **LORD** our **Lord**, how excellent is thy name in all the earth" (Psalm 8:1). LORD is used in combination with Healer (Exodus 15:26), Provider (Gen. 22:14), and Shepherd (Psalm 23:1). In each of these combinations, the LORD revealed to Israel what he would do for them. When Lord is used, Israel listened for him to tell them what they were to do. The two, **LORD** and **Lord,** form the covenant relationship: **Lord—Wisdom + LORD—Promise = Covenant.**

In Isaiah 6:1–8, both **LORD** and **Lord** are used: "Holy, holy, holy, is the **LORD** of hosts." Being in the presence of the LORD's holiness, Isaiah acknowledges his own sinfulness and cries out for cleansing. Immediately after his cleansing, he hears the voice of the **Lord** saying: "Whom shall I send, and who will go for us?" He answers, "Here am I; send me." These verses of

Scripture clarify for us one of the reasons for telling the **LORD** what to do for us and others rather than listening for the **Lord** to tell us what to do—not seeing our sinfulness in the presence of the **LORD's** holiness.

Following the healing of the lame man at the temple, Peter and John taught the people and preached in Jesus the resurrection from the dead. The Sadducees were greatly disturbed at their preaching and teaching and put them in custody. The next day they were released and commanded not to speak at all nor teach in the name of Jesus.

When they were let go, they joined the other believers and reported all that the chief priests and elders had said to them. So when they heard that, they raised their voice to God with one accord and said: "Lord, thou art God, which hast made heaven, and earth, and the sea..." (Acts 4:1–24). The word translated "Lord" in Acts 4:24 is Δέσποτα [des-pot-ah]. The same word was used by Paul for slave owners, and the word translated servants, δούλοις [doo-lois] in Acts 4:29 is translated "slaves" (I Tim. 6:1; Titus 2:9).

The believers acknowledged themselves as slaves of the Master without any rights. They were obeying the Lord's commands: "If anyone desires to come after Me, let him deny himself, and take up his cross, and follow Me. For whoever desires to save his life will lose it, but whoever loses his life for My sake will find it" (Matt. 16:24, 25 NKJV). They were presenting themselves as living sacrifices to be used by him in whatever way he chose regardless of the costs. They had experienced the holiness of the Lord as Isaiah had. They were all filled with the Holy Spirit and were ready to serve.

After Paul met the Lord on the road to Damascus, the first words he spoke were, "Lord, what wilt thou have me to do?" (Acts 9:6) The remainder of his life was lived in anticipation of the answer to that question regardless of the sacrifice or suffering, and they were many (2 Cor. 4:7–12).

Prayer Bloopers

Several years ago my wife and I were on vacation with some friends, and one of them bought a book of *Bulletin Bloopers*. We all got lots of laughs while we were traveling and listening to someone read the bloopers. The people who made the bloopers didn't know they were making them. I had been practicing the Chosen Fast several months before discovering that I was making prayer bloopers. The Chosen Fast revolutionized the way I pray. I was asking instead of giving thanks. Rather than listening for him to tell me what to do, I was asking him to do what he had promised to do.

Lord, Comfort Them.

One day while praying, I asked the Lord to comfort a person who was going through a difficult trial. No sooner had I made the request, and 2 Corinthians 1:3–4 came to my mind: "Blessed be God, even the Father of our Lord Jesus Christ, the Father of mercies, and God of all comfort; who comforteth us in all our tribulation, that we may be able to comfort them which are in any trouble, by the comfort wherewith we ourselves are comforted of God" (2 Cor. 1:3, 4). Instead of asking the Lord to do what he was doing, I should have thanked him for comforting the person. Not only that, but I was asking him to do what the Holy Spirit had given me a gift to do—comfort the person (Rom. 12:8).

The word translated comfort in 2 Corinthians 1:3 is also translated encouragement in Romans 12:8 and Hebrew 3:13. The KJV translates the word "exhortation" in 2 Corinthians 12:8 and Hebrews 3:13, but "comfort" in 2 Corinthians 1:3. That prayer blooper got me thinking about my praying, and I noticed myself making several prayer bloopers.

Lord, Save Them.

Shortly after that I was praying, and I asked the Lord to save a certain person. Immediately after asking, John 3:16 came to my mind. "For God so loved the world, that he gave his only begotten Son, that whoever believeth in him should not perish, but have everlasting life." Then I recognized the prayer blooper. I didn't have to ask the Lord to save the person. That is why he sent his Son into the world. Instead of asking him to save the person, I needed to thank him for all that he has done and is doing to save the person.

While I am thanking the Lord for all he is doing to save someone, I need to be asking myself some questions: What am I doing to share the "Good News" of salvation through the crucifixion and resurrection of Jesus Christ with others? What am I doing to show God's love to people in need of salvation? How much am I giving to missions? How much am I giving to help the unsaved in my community and around the world? How much of my income goes for my needs and pleasure in comparison to what I give to fulfill the Great Commission (Matt. 28:18–20)?

God has reconciled us to himself through Jesus Christ and has given to us the ministry of reconciliation. The work of reconciliation he did through Jesus Christ he now does through Jesus Christ in us (2 Cor. 5:18). He fills us with the Holy Spirit to be his witnesses (Acts 1:8). I was asking him to do what he has equipped me to do—fulfill the Great Commission.

Lord, Heal Them.

Another prayer blooper was asking the Lord to heal people. I don't have to ask the Lord to heal anyone or myself. He is the Healer (Ex. 15:26). He heals people. Rather than asking him to do something he is doing, I need to give him thanks for what he is doing—healing people. The Holy Spirit gives gifts of healings (1 Cor. 12:9). Gifts of healings are given to every believer (Mark 16:18; 1 Cor. 12:7). The gifts of the Spirit are God's grace (Rom. 12:6). In the Greek New Testament, the same noun χάρις [khar-ece] is used for both grace and gratitude. In the following verses, χάρις is translated thanks: Rom. 7:25; 6:17; 1 Cor.15:57; 2 Cor. 9:15; Heb. 12:28. We receive grace form God as a gift, and "thank you" is grace from us to God for the gift. It is grace for grace. Giving and receiving grace is fellowship with God.

Healing is a gift (1 Cor. 12:9). A gift isn't earned by fasting and prayer, the number of people praying, the words we use, or how much faith we have. It is a gift to the saved and the unsaved, those who have faith and those who don't have faith. The Lord is the healer (Ex. 15:26), and he is no respecter of persons (Acts 10:34). He sends rain on the just and the unjust (Matt. 5:45).

Not only was I asking him to do what he was doing, but I was asking a number of people to join me in prayer for the sick. Then I realized my error. Why did I have to get as many people as possible to pray for the sick? He is the Healer and gives gifts of healings. Instead of getting several people to pray in order for the Lord to heal the sick, I needed to invite people to unite with me in thanksgiving to the Lord for the grace, mercy, love, comfort, and healing he is giving the sick.

In the body of Christ, as in the human body, when one of the members suffers, all the members suffer (1 Cor. 12:26). Several times I have accidently hit my thumb with a hammer, and instantly my whole body knew it. Likewise in the body of Christ, the Church, when one member suffers, all of the body shares in the suffering. Our love and compassion go out to them; we support them through our prayers in agreement for their healing in the name of Jesus and give thanks for the gift of healing. But in addition to that, we also listen for the Lord to give us a word of wisdom that tells us how we are to minister to them in their time of sickness—send a card, mow the lawn, take care of the children, take food, visit, etc.

Consider for a moment this scenario: On his son's birthday, the father with a big smile on his face offers his son a beautifully wrapped gift. But rather than accepting the gift joyfully and with thanksgiving, the son begins to plead with the father to give him the gift. He cries and asks his friends to join him in asking his father for the gift. So his friends join him in crying and asking the father to give the gift to the son. Then the son begins to tell the father all the things he will do if he gives him the gift.

What would the father be thinking while standing there with his hand outstretched offering the gift to his son, but instead of receiving it, he and his friends are crying and pleading for it? Isn't that ridiculous? But isn't that the way we respond to our heavenly Father offering us the gifts of healings? Instead of receiving them with thanksgiving, we plead for them, and try to earn them by bargaining with God and telling him all we will do if he will heal us.

Asking the Lord to do what he has told us in his Word he will do is having a false concept of God. We treat him as if he doesn't know what is going on, as if we have to get his attention. We plead with him to do what we fail to realize he is already doing. We miss God's grace and try to gain his favor by works. He is the Creator, Redeemer, and Savior of the world. He is not a "grandfather" in heaven that must be awakened and told what to do.

Lord, Be with Them.

Another prayer blooper was asking the Lord to be with people. I don't have to ask the Lord to be with anyone. We can't escape his presence. David wrote, "Whither shall I go from thy spirit? or whither shall I flee from thy presence? If I ascend up into heaven, thou art there: if I make my bed in hell, behold thou art there. If I take the wings of the morning, and dwell in the uttermost parts of the sea; Even there shall thy hand lead me, and thy right hand shall hold me" (Psalm 139:7–10). "He will never leave us or forsake us" (Heb. 13:5). "I am with you always, even until the end of the world" (Matt. 28:18–20). Why did I ask him to be with them? I was missing the reality of God being with me as well as everywhere.

Lord, Bless Them.

"Lord, bless them" was another one of my prayer bloopers. He blesses everyone, both the evil and the good. He gives to all breath and life and all things (Acts 17:25). David understood that truth when he wrote, "Bless the LORD, O my soul; and all that is within me, bless his holy name. Bless the Lord, O my soul, and forget not all His benefits: Who forgiveth all thine iniquities; who healeth all thy diseases; Who redeemeth thy life from destruction; who crowneth thee with loving-kindness and tender mercies; Who satisfieth thy mouth with good things; so that thy youth is renewed like the eagle's" (Psalm 103:1–5). David set a standard for us—

instead of asking the Lord to bless us and others, thank him for his blessings.

A Christian is a priest (I Peter 2:9; Rev. 1:5, 6). That which Peter wrote of Christians being priests was also spoken of Israel (Ex. 19:5, 6). The priests were to bless the people (Num. 6:24–26). New Testament priests bless others by making them rich. Paul wrote that he was poor, yet making many rich (2 Cor. 6:9). What he wrote of himself, he wrote of Jesus. "For you know the grace of our Lord Jesus Christ, that though He was rich, yet for your sakes He became poor, that you through His poverty might become rich" (2 Cor. 8:9 NKJV). When Paul wrote about the poverty of Jesus, he was referring to his crucifixion and resurrection. There are three sources of riches to bless others: **the ransom of a person's life, the kingdom of heaven, and wisdom.**

It is through the crucifixion and resurrection of Jesus Christ that our life can be redeemed. In Proverbs 13:8, we read: "The ransom of a man's life is his riches." That verse helps us to better understand the words of Jesus and the redemption of our life: "For what shall it profit a man, if he shall gain the whole world, and lose his own soul? Or what shall a man give in exchange for his soul?" (Mark 8:36, 37). Through the poverty of our Lord Jesus Christ, we are rich—redeemed. We are priests; we bless others by sharing with them our testimony of deliverance from the slavery of sin and death, to a life of righteousness and life.

"The kingdom of heaven is like unto treasure hid in a field, the which when a man hath found, and hideth, and for joy thereof goeth and selleth all that he hath, and buyeth that field" (Matt. 13:44). When we discover the kingdom of heaven, we have found something more valuable than anything we have or desire. We sell all we have and buy it. We have a complete change of value and perspective. It is only when we experience that change of value and perspective that we can understand the teaching of Jesus in the Sermon on the Mount. "But seek ye first the kingdom of God, and His righteousness; and all these things shall be added unto you" (Matt. 6:33).

Finding the treasure in the field is experiencing the kingdom of heaven, heaven on earth. That was what the Lord intended for Israel. He dwelt in the tabernacle. It was heaven on earth. He was their King, and he gave them the Ten Commandments as the standard for living in his kingdom. Jesus gave us the new commandment as a standard for living in the kingdom of heaven. "A new commandment I give unto you, that ye love one another; as I have loved you, that ye also love one another" (John 13:34). The new commandment fulfills the law (Rom. 13:8).

Keeping his commandments is wisdom, and wisdom is better than rubies, and all the things one may desire cannot be compared with her (Proverbs 8:11). It is through discipleship that the New Testament priest grows in wisdom. Just before he ascended back to the Father, Jesus said, "All authority has been given to Me in heaven and on earth. Go therefore and make disciples of all nations, baptizing them in the name of the Father and of the Son and of the Holy Spirit, teaching them to observe all things that I have commanded you; and lo, I am with you always, even to the end of the age" (Matt. 28:18–20 NKJV).

The first disciples were to teach others what the Lord had taught them, and that process was to continue until he returns. All authority in heaven and earth is with the disciples as they make disciples because Jesus is with them. He is with them until he returns!

The disciples are taught and are to teach. To teach is to live what they have been taught—make others rich through wisdom. Every disciple is to live and teach what Jesus taught the first disciples. One way of teaching is the classroom. But that is not the only way. Very few disciples teach that way. For discipleship to be effective, it must take place outside the classroom of the church building to the classroom of the home, school, workplace, etc.

Evangelism and discipleship can be defined as "poor, yet making many rich." Evangelism is sharing the riches of redemption and the kingdom of heaven, and discipleship is sharing the riches of wisdom. Paul wrote to Timothy, "Command those who are rich in this present age not to be haughty, nor to trust in uncertain riches but in the living God, who gives us richly all things to enjoy. Let them do good, that they may be **rich in good works**, ready to give, willing to share, storing up for themselves a good foundation for the time to come, that they may lay hold on eternal life" (I Tim. 6:17–19). It is the person who has the riches of redemption, the kingdom of heaven, and wisdom that is **rich in good works**.

Lord, Help Them.

Asking the Lord to help people was another prayer blooper. I don't have to ask the Lord to help people. He is the Helper. "Thou art the helper of the fatherless" (Psalm 10:14). "Behold, God is my helper" (Psalm 54:4). "The Lord is my helper, and I will not fear what man shall do to me" (Heb.13:6). Rather than ask him to help someone, I need to humble myself and receive the gift of helps—αντιλημψεις [an-til-ape-sis] (I Cor. 12:28). The gift of helps is giving assistance, ministry to the sick and needy. It is exercised by members of the church for the benefit of one another (Rom.12:7). The house of Stephanus devoted themselves to ministry to the saints (ICor. 16:15).

A word of knowledge and word of wisdom are given to those who make themselves available to ex-ercise the gift of helps. Through the gifts of a word of knowledge and a word of wisdom the Holy Spirit makes known to us those who are in need of helps and what we are to do for them.

The gift of ministry can't be separated from the gift of helps, and every believer is to be equipped for the work of ministry (Eph. 4:11, 12). To the one who is given the gift of helps is also given the gift of giving, show-ing mercy, encouraging, teaching, healings, miracles, etc. These gifts aren't reserved for the pastors and evan-gelists during the worship service on Sunday morning; they are for the disciples 24/7/365. The gift of helps is the love of God in action; it is love for the neighbor. The gift of helps is God at work in us. There is no Chosen Fast without the gift of helps.

Our praying reveals our understanding or lack of understanding of the Lord. To avoid prayer bloopers, I have started observing my prayers. I have found the best way to avoid prayer bloopers, making the Lord our servant with less intelligence than we have, is to give him thanks for what he does which is his will for our life (1 Thess. 5:17).

Asking

We don't stop asking when we practice the Chosen Fast. We are invited to ask. "Ask, and it shall be given you" (Matt. 7:7). But instead of asking the Lord to do for us or others what he has said he will do, we ask what he wants us to do. *Lord, where do you want me to live? What do you want me to do in order to earn a living that glorifies you? Where do you want me to go to school? Where do you want me to work? Whom do you want me to marry? Where do you want me to go to church?* The asking is to serve the Lord.

He invites us to ask for wisdom. "If any of you lack wisdom, let him ask of God, that giveth to all liberally, and upbraideth not, and it shall be given him" (James 1:5). In a dream, the Lord invited King Solomon to ask for whatever he wished. He asked for wisdom to judge the people righteously (2 Chron. 1:7–12). The Lord granted Solomon's request. He became one of the wisest men who ever lived. However, asking for wisdom isn't a substitute for discipleship. Our asking may very well reveal our lack of discipleship—searching for wisdom as hidden treasure (Proverbs 2:4).

Soon after I was saved, I asked the Lord what he would have me do. I was asking for wisdom. He revealed to me in my spirit that I was to be a pastor. Soon thereafter, I acted upon the answer and started preparing for pastoral ministry.

When we repent of our sins and trust in the death and resurrection of Jesus Christ to save us, we are forgiven of our sins. We receive the Holy Spirit, the Spirit of God. God dwells in us. He knows the thoughts of our heart, our mind, before we speak. Not only does he know what we are thinking, he speaks to our spirit. We are continually having a conversation together. We soon discover that prayer is not a monologue, talking to God, but a dialogue, thanking him for all he is doing and listening for him to tell us what we are to do.

I experienced the fear of the LORD while reading through the Bible before I knew Jesus Christ as my Savior and Lord. The fear of the LORD is the beginning of wisdom (Proverbs 9:10). From first grade through high school, I had very little interest in any subject. I didn't like school, and my grades expressed it. I passed, and that was all I was expecting. In order to complete high school, I transferred to the vocational school my last two years. Had it not been for vocational school, I probably wouldn't have graduated.

On the first day in vocational school, the instructor informed us that by choosing vocational school we could never qualify for college. I thought, *so what? I have no desire to go to college.* I wanted to finish high school, get a job, and make some money so that I could buy the things I wanted. But after I experienced the fear of the Lord, the beginning of wisdom, I had a desire to learn.

When I was in school, I detested history, math, and English. But after being born again, I had a desire to learn history, math, and English. I had a desire to go to college and earn a degree. Even though the teacher at the vocational school told us we would never be able to enroll in college, I believed the Lord would make a way. I not only wanted to graduate from college, but I wanted to graduate from seminary. I was twenty-eight, married, and the father of two daughters who were both in school.

I tried to come up with a solution, but I had no success. Then I asked the Lord for wisdom, and he revealed to me step by step what I was to do in order to go to college and graduate. I lived about twenty miles from Marietta College, but with the classes I had taken and my grades there was no way I could ever enroll in Marietta College. Then in the fall of 1962, I saw an ad in the evening paper that Marietta College was offering night classes. There were no questions about transcript of grades. I was excited, but I was afraid to try. After the classes started, I realized the Lord had opened the door, and I had failed to take advantage of the opportunity. I was sorry and repented of my failure. The failure gave me the determination to enroll in January, which I did.

My vocabulary was so limited that I had to have a dictionary in one hand and the textbook in the other in order to read the textbook. But I passed the course with a good grade and made plans to enroll in two classes the following fall. After completing them, I enrolled in three classes the following spring and also completed a course in summer school. I was able to complete three years of college in four years by attending night school and summer school while working a full time job and pastoring a church.

In the fall of 1967, I made application to attend full time. The admission staff looked over my college grades and discovered that I had completed all the required courses with good grades. I was admitted as a full-time student and graduated in May of '68. It was the Lord giving me wisdom that made the impossible possible. After graduating from college, I enrolled in seminary for the fall class of '68 and graduated with a Master of Divinity degree in May of '71. I was ordained in June of '72. With wisdom from the Lord, dreams do come true even when we're told they are impossible.

We need to always remember that he is all powerful, all knowing, and ever present. He is Lord, and we are his servants. Instead of telling him what to do, we are to listen for him to tell us what we are to do. I have found in my own life that when I hear from him and do what he says, I am successful. But when I make the decisions and ask him to help, I fail. However, when I made the wrong decision and failed, the Lord did not forsake me. I paid dearly for making the wrong decision, but he never gave up on me. He gave me another chance.

Listening

A disciple named Ananias was listening when the Lord said to him in a vision, "Ananias." He answered; "Behold, I am here, Lord" (Acts 9:10). Then the Lord asked Ananias to go to the house where Saul was staying. Ananias was fearful of going; he had heard about all the evil Saul had done to the saints at Jerusalem and knew he had come to Damascus to do the same. But the Lord said to Ananias, "Go thy way: for he is a chosen vessel unto me, to bear my name before the Gentiles, and kings, and the children of Israel: For I will shew him how great things he must suffer for my name's sake" (Acts 9:15, 16).

Ananias obeyed the Lord; he went to Saul and said, "Brother Saul, the Lord, even Jesus, that appeared unto thee in the way as thou camest, hath sent me, that thou mightiest receive thy sight, and be filled with the Holy Ghost" (Acts 9:17). Ananias was listening for the Lord to speak, and when he did, Ananias obeyed. Had Ananias not been listening, he would have missed one of the most important ministries of his life. Because he was listening and obeyed, his name has been read by millions down through the centuries in the best-selling book of all time—the Bible.

There is an account of an unnamed prophet in 1 Kings 13. He started out just as Ananias did; he heard the Lord speaking to him, and he obeyed the voice of the Lord. He went to Bethel and prophesied at the altar of burnt incense where King Jeroboam was standing. He prophesied of the birth of King Josiah and the reforms he would bring to Israel. He gave a sign saying, "This is the sign which the LORD hath spoken; Behold, the altar shall be rent, and the ashes that are upon it shall be poured out."

When Jeroboam heard the saying of the man of God, he put forth his hand and gave a command to lay hold of the prophet. The hand which he put forth against the prophet was then paralyzed. The altar was also broken, and the ashes poured out from the altar according to the sign that the man of God had given by the word of the Lord. Then the king asked the prophet to pray for the Lord to restore his hand. He did, and the king's hand was restored.

After the king's hand was restored, he invited the prophet to go home with him and refresh himself, and he would give him a gift. The prophet answered the king, "If thou wilt give me half thine house, I will not go in with thee, neither will I eat bread nor drink water in this place: For so was it charged me by the word of the LORD, saying, Eat no bread, nor drink water, nor turn again by the same way that thou camest. So he went another way, and returned not by the way that he came to Bethel."

An old prophet dwelt in Bethel, and his sons came and told him all that the prophet had done that day in Bethel. Then the old prophet went after the man of God and found him sitting under an oak tree. He invited him to his home to eat, and the man of God told the old prophet the same as he told the king. Then the old prophet lied to him and said an angel had spoken to him by the word of the Lord, saying, "Bring him back with thee into thine house, that he may eat bread and drink water." The man of God believed the lie, went back with the old prophet, ate bread, and drank water.

While the man of God was eating bread and drinking water, the old prophet cried out saying, "Forasmuch as thou hast disobeyed the mouth of the Lord, and hast not kept the commandment which the LORD thy God commanded thee, But camest back, and hast eaten bread and drunk water in the place, of the which the LORD did say to thee, Eat no bread, and drink no water; thy carcase shall not come into the sepulcher of thy fathers." As the man of God was returning to Judah, a lion attacked and killed him. An unusual spectacle followed his death—the donkey he was riding stood by his slain body as well as the lion that killed him.

The prophet from Judah wasn't given a name because he disobeyed the commandment of the Lord and was slain. Had he obeyed, he would have been given a name. He could have been one of the greatest prophets in the Old Testament. He started out well; he heard and obeyed the voice of the Lord. Then he heard a voice that wasn't from the Lord. He obeyed it and lost his life, but his prophecy concerning Josiah and his reforms came true as he had prophesied. This account is a vital lesson for every Christian. We must always be watchful and distinguish the voice of the Lord from our own voice or other voices.

God spoke to the fathers through the prophets and has spoken to us in the last days through his Son (Heb. 1:1, 2). One of the best ways to become familiar with the voice of his Son, our Shepherd, is reading and obeying the Scriptures. Knowing the voice of the Shepherd by listening to his voice as we read the Scriptures and obeying what he says prepares us to recognize his voice when he speaks to us in the still small voice to minister to others. A person who says he hears from God and doesn't read and obey his voice in the Scriptures may very well be hearing his own voice or one of the other voices out there. How many Christians have fallen into the same error as the unnamed prophet from Judah?

From time to time, we read in the newspaper or hear on the news about someone who says he or she heard God telling them to kill another person. It is evident the person wasn't familiar with the voice of the Shepherd but heard their own voice or another voice. Such accounts have resulted in many people being skeptical of anyone who says he or she heard from the Lord. Jesus said his sheep follow him for they know his voice (John 10:4). When we follow the Shepherd, he leads us in the paths of righteousness for his name's sake (Psalm 23:3).

God spoke to people in the Old Testament: Adam, Noah, Abraham, Isaac, Jacob, Joshua, Moses, Samuel, David, Elijah, Elisha, and all the prophets. In the New Testament, he spoke to Mary, Joseph, John the Baptist, Peter, Paul, John, etc. At the Day of Pentecost, the apostles spoke to the people gathered from all nations as the Spirit gave them words to speak.

Prayer isn't a monologue but a dialogue. It is talking and listening. Prayer, a monologue, talking to God and not receiving an answer, is like talking to an idol that doesn't speak. God hears and answers. He speaks to us through the Scriptures, and when we hear and do what he says, we are talking with God. It is a dialogue. It is fellowship with God. He brings to our remembrance. He speaks to us in dreams and visions. He gives us words to speak in times of trials (Mark 13:11). He gives us words of wisdom, knowledge, prophecy, tongues, interpretation (I Cor. 12:8, 10). The words in each of the gifts are from him. His Spirit bears witness with our spirit that we are the children of God (Rom. 8:16).

God dwells in the hearts of his people and knows their thoughts. We don't have to speak in an audible voice for him to hear us. Likewise, he doesn't have to speak in an audible voice for us to hear him. He speaks to our spirit. Listening for the Lord to speak to us is praying. He may speak at any time. If we aren't listening, we may very well miss the opportunity of a lifetime. Therefore in order to practice the Chosen Fast, which is 24/7/365, prayer can't be confined to a designated time such as five, ten, or fifteen minutes jam-packed into a tight schedule. The 24/7/365 may be something like 10% for asking, 40% for thanksgiving, and 50% for listening. That is how we are able to pray without ceasing (I Thess. 5:17).

Listening is essential in order to practice the Chosen Fast. The Holy Spirit will make known ministries that we may overlook, opportunities to minister and the blessings accompanying the ministry. It is the first fruits of the resurrection—priests of God and of Christ (Rev. 20:6). It is life in the marvelous light (I Peter 2:9). It is the kingdom of heaven (Matt. 5:3).

After I was justified by faith, I heard the Lord calling me into the pastoral ministry. I was obedient to the
call, and he prospered me. The Greek New Testament
word ευοδουσθαι [yoo-od-ooce-thah-ee] is translated
"prosper" in 3 John 2. Its literal sense is "be led along
a good road."[5] In the Septuagint, the Greek translation
of the Hebrew Old Testament, the same word is translated both "prosperous" and "good success" in Joshua
1:8. "This book of the law shall not depart out of thy
mouth, but thou shalt meditate therein day and night,
that thou mayest observe to do according to all that is
written therein: for then thou shall make thy way prosperous, and then thou shalt have good success."

Taking the literal sense of ευοδουσθαι, Joseph
was prosperous when he was a slave in the house of
Potiphar, and he was prosperous when he was in prison as well as when he was governor over all of Egypt
(Gen. 37–50). He was prosperous in each because the
Lord was leading him along a good road—the paths of
righteousness (Psalm 23:3). The Lord was leading Joseph in the way to save Jacob's family and the Egyptians.
Therefore, Joseph could say to his brothers, "Do not
be afraid, for am I in the place of God? But as for you,
you meant evil against me; but God meant it for good,
in order to bring it about as it is this day, to save many
people alive" (Gen. 50:19–21 NKJV).

Paul and Silas were prosperous when they were
beaten and put in the inner prison with their feet secure
in the stocks (Acts 16:22–24). It was through that experience that the jailer and his whole family were saved.
When we give the same definition to the word prosper

in 3 John 2 or Joshua 1:8 as the twenty-first century, secular, materialistic worldview, we miss much of the Old and New Testament meanings.

Job's friends had a materialistic understanding of prosperity and didn't understand the true meaning of prosperity as was experienced by Job when he lost all his material wealth. The same was true of Asaph when he observed the prosperity of the wicked (Psalm 73:3). He said, "Surely I have cleansed my heart in vain, and washed my hands in innocence. For all day long I have been plagued, and chastened every morning" (v. 13, 14 NKJV). He was ready to give up his faith. Then he went into the sanctuary of God and understood their end. He confessed that he was foolish and ignorant. He understood true prosperity—"You will guide me with Your counsel, and afterward receive me to glory" (v. 24).

Even while my heavenly Father was prospering me in the pastoral ministry, there were other things I wanted to do, and I took the desire to do them as the voice of the Lord. I obeyed my voice. My heavenly Father knew what was best for me when he called me into the pastoral ministry. But I stepped out of his call and did what I wanted to do rather than what he had called me to do. It was a disaster. I suffered dearly, physically, mentally, spiritually, and financially. I would have gone under, but in my disobedience, he had mercy on me.

From my late teens, I had the idea of working with youth on a farm. During the mid-1970s while pastoring a church, I gave a lot of thought to buying a farm and using it as a place to minister to youth. I never found the right farm, but in August of '84, I saw an ad in the newspaper for house parents on a farm for troubled youth. I thought, *This is just what I have been looking for, and I don't have to buy the farm.* I applied for the position with great anticipation. I thanked the Lord for the opportunity and prayed that my wife and I would be hired for the position.

We were invited for an interview. When we arrived at the farm, I was happy to see that it was more than I had visualized. It was a large scenic farm situated among rolling hills and meadows with mountains in the background. A few days after the interview, I received word that we had been accepted. I was delighted. I resigned the church where I was pastor and moved the middle of September of '84.

It only took a few hours as house parents to realize I had made a blunder. I wanted out, but it was too late. The Lord hadn't called me to work with troubled youth. It is a very important ministry, but it requires a special calling. It wasn't my calling. I started praying and asking the Lord to help me get out, but the country was in a recession. Jobs were difficult to find. I had asked instead of listening, and I was paying the consequences. I was like Jonah; I ran away from my calling, and I was swallowed up.

From my late teens, I had wanted to be a real estate broker. During the winter of 1985, I decided to get my real estate license while working with troubled youth. Also for a number of years, I had thought about church planting. So I decided to try both—selling real estate and planting a church. I passed my real estate examination in April of '85, resigned from my position with troubled youth, and moved to the area where I was going to plant the church.

I went from the "frying pan into the fire." There is a vast difference between pastoring an established church and planting a church. Church planting is a special calling. I wasn't called to be a real estate broker or plant a church. I was in double trouble. Selling real estate is interesting and challenging. It helps people make the major investment of their life and helps them achieve their goal, home ownership. I was trying to do two things that weren't my calling.

The Lord was merciful to me and helped me plant the church. I sold some property, which helped me survive. For seven years that was all I did—survive. I am thankful I survived. There were times when I didn't have money to pay my income tax in April. Another time I didn't have money to pay my car insurance or personal property tax. I couldn't afford health insurance, and I relied totally upon the Lord for the gifts of healing. One Easter my wife and I didn't have money for groceries. Then a couple of friends called and asked me to perform their marriage ceremony. I did, and they gave me an honorarium. It was enough to buy food for Easter dinner and the following week.

The year I didn't have money for car insurance or personal property tax (which had to be paid before I could get the car insurance), I prayed and asked the Lord to give me a sale to pay the car insurance and taxes. But he didn't; each time I asked him, I received the same answer, "Go to the bank and borrow the money."

I thought, *it is foolish to go to the bank and borrow money. I don't have enough income to get a loan.*

After a few days and no money, the insurance was running out. I was desperate. So I went to the bank to ask for a loan. As I was on my way, I thought, *this is foolish.* But when I got to the bank and asked for the loan, I was surprised when the loan officer didn't ask for my present income but the income of the previous year. She asked me to bring in my federal tax return for the previous year. I did; within an hour, I had the money. I did what the Lord asked me to do, and I got the money. I am thankful the Lord didn't give up on me in my disobedience. He had mercy upon me and made a way when it looked as though there was no way. After that, I started getting more sales.

In January of 1991, I resigned from the church after six years and sold real estate full time. I enjoyed selling real estate so much that I decided not to pastor again. Then in June of 1992, the desire to pastor was rebirthed in my heart, and the Lord opened a door for me to pastor again. After serving as an interim pastor in the summer of 1992, I was elected as senior pastor in August of 1992. The Lord restored me to my first calling. I am so thankful he did.

Chapter 6
The Chosen Fast—
Matthew 25

Jesus said the kingdom of heaven will be like ten virgins. Five were wise and five were foolish. The wise were disciples who delighted in hearing the instructions and obeying them. They were doers of the word and not hearers only. They were ready when they heard the midnight cry: "Behold the bridegroom cometh; go ye out to meet him" (Matt. 25:6). They lit their lamps and went to meet him.

Unlike the wise who were ready, the foolish weren't ready; they didn't have oil in their lamps. Therefore, instead of going out to meet the bridegroom, they had to go and buy oil for their lamps. While they were going to buy oil, the bridegroom came; and the wise went with him to the marriage feast, and the door was shut. "Afterwards came the foolish saying, Lord, Lord, open the door to us. But he answered and said, Verily I say unto you, I know you not" (Matt. 25:11, 12).

Those who practice the Chosen Fast are the wise that hear the sayings of Jesus and do them. They build their house upon the rock (Matt. 7:24). They are the wise who know that nothing compares in value to wisdom, and they search for it as hidden treasure (Proverbs

2:4). They are disciples making disciples (Matt. 28:18–20). Jesus makes his home with them (John 14:23). He knows them.

Jesus compared the kingdom of heaven to a businessman going on a long trip. He gave money to his servants to invest and make a profit while he was gone. He gave them money according to their ability, and he took his trip. Two of the servants invested and doubled the money they were given. But one of the servants hid the money rather than investing it. After a long time the businessman returned and settled accounts with them.

The two who doubled his money brought it to him, and he said to each of them, "Well done, thou good and faithful servant: thou hast been faithful over a few things, I will make thee ruler over many things: enter thou into the joy of thy lord" (Matt. 25:21). But he called the one who hadn't invested his money a wicked and lazy servant. The money was taken from him and given to the servant who made the largest investment and gained the most money. Then he said to cast the unprofitable servant into the outer darkness, where there will be weeping and gnashing of teeth (Matt. 25:26–30).

Peter wrote, "As each one has received a gift, minister it to one another, as stewards of the manifold grace of God. If anyone speaks, let him speak as the oracles of God. If anyone ministers, let him do it as with the ability which God supplies, that in all things God may be glorified through Jesus Christ, to whom belong the glory and the dominion forever and ever. Amen" (1 Peter 4:10, 11 NKJV).

God's grace comes to us as a gift (see Rom. 12:6–8). Just as the businessman gave money to his servants to invest and give account of it, the Holy Spirit gives each of us gifts to minister to others, and we will have to give an account of it. Practicing the Chosen Fast is investing the gifts of grace, the gifts of the Holy Spirit—ministry, exhortation, giving, showing mercy (Rom. 12:6–8), word of wisdom, word of knowledge, faith, healings, working of miracles, discerning of spirits, and helps (I Cor. 12:8–10, 28). We are laying up treasure in heaven (Luke 18:22) and building upon the foundation gold, silver, and precious stones which will not be burned up at the Judgment Seat of Christ (I Cor. 3:9–15).

The ministries in Matthew 25:35–36 are very similar to the ministries in the Chosen Fast (Isaiah 58:6–8, 9b, 10a). Those who minister the gifts are called blessed and invited to inherit the kingdom prepared for them from the foundation of the world (Matt. 25:34). But those who don't minister the gifts are called cursed, and they are told to depart into everlasting fire prepared for the devil and his angels (Matt. 25:41). The chapter concludes by saying those who didn't minister the gifts will go away into everlasting punishment, but the righteous go into life eternal (Matt. 25:46).

"Blessed are the poor in spirit: for theirs is the kingdom of heaven" (Matt. 5:3) is a good description of the righteous in Matthew 25:35–36. They are the poor in spirit who have found the treasure hidden in the field and sold all and purchased the field (Matt. 13:44). They are poor making many rich (2 Cor. 6:10). They are slaves claiming no rights for themselves in order to serve the

Master no matter what the sacrifice may be (Acts 4:23–31). They receive the gift of helps and minister to those in need (Matt. 25:35, 36).

When we read of the Lord's coming in the New Testament, we are given instruction of how we are to live until he comes. That is the message of Matthew 25. Practicing the Chosen Fast is watching for his coming—living in the kingdom of heaven until the Son of Man comes in his glory, and all the holy angels with him (Matt. 25:31). Begin the Chosen Fast, and enjoy the life of the age to come before it arrives.

Endnotes

[1] George Arthur Buttrick, et al., *The Interpreter's Dictionary of the Bible*, Volume 1 (Nashville: Abingdon, 1980) 150-151.

[2] Randy Hurst, "The Suffering Church," *Pentecostal Evangel*, 4 Oct. 2009: 12, 15.

[3] Robert P. Holland, *Some Understand 1 + 6 = 7* (Baltimore: PublishAmerica, 2010) 10-11.

[4] Holland 23.

[5] William F. Arndt and F. Wilbur Gingrich, *A Greek-English Lexicon of the New Testament and Other Early Christian Literature* (Chicago: The University of Chicago Press, 1957) 324.

About the Author

Robert P. Holland completed a Master of Divinity from MTSO, a bachelor's degree from Marietta College, and is an ordained minister with the Assemblies of God. He served as senior pastor from 1965 until 2002 and since then as associate pastor. He is a faculty member of the Appalachian District School of Ministry (AD-SOM), teaching the Pentateuch, Romans, Eschatology, and Psalms. Robert's first book, *Some Understand 1 + 6 = 7*, was published in October, 2010 and he is currently working on his third book, *The Wisdom and Promise Study Bible*, which he plans to publish in the fall of 2012. He and his wife Dolly, also an ordained minister, have been married fifty-seven years and have two married daughters, three grandchildren, and two great grandchildren. Robert and Dolly enjoy practicing the *Chosen Fast* and living on their wildlife refuge.

CPSIA information can be obtained at www.ICGtesting.com
Printed in the USA
LVOW102259280113

317574LV00021B/645/P